ISBN 978-1-330-08242-3
PIBN 10021289

1 MONTH OF
FREE
READING

at

www.ForgottenBooks.com

By purchasing this book you are eligible for one month membership to ForgottenBooks.com, giving you unlimited access to our entire collection of over 1,000,000 titles via our web site and mobile apps.

To claim your free month visit:

www.forgottenbooks.com/free21289

English
Français
Deutsche
Italiano
Español
Português

www.forgottenbooks.com

Mythology Photography **Fiction** Fishing Christianity **Art** Cooking Essays Buddhism Freemasonry Medicine **Biology** Music **Ancient Egypt** Evolution Carpentry Physics Dance Geology **Mathematics** Fitness Shakespeare **Folklore** Yoga Marketing **Confidence** Immortality Biographies Poetry **Psychology** Witchcraft Electronics Chemistry History **Law** Accounting **Philosophy** Anthropology Alchemy Drama Quantum Mechanics Atheism Sexual Health **Ancient History** **Entrepreneurship** Languages Sport Paleontology Needlework Islam **Metaphysics** Investment Archaeology Parenting Statistics Criminology **Motivational**

WORK AND WAGES

THE REWARD OF LABOUR AND
THE COST OF WORK

FOUNDED ON THE EXPERIENCES OF
THE LATE MR. BRASSEY

BY

EARL BRASSEY, G.C.B.

A VOLUME OF EXTRACTS,
REVISED, AND PARTIALLY REWRITTEN

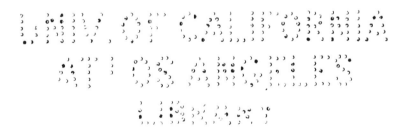

LONGMANS, GREEN AND CO.
39 PATERNOSTER ROW, LONDON
FOURTH AVENUE & 30TH STREET, NEW YORK
BOMBAY, CALCUTTA, AND MADRAS
1916

PREFACE

THE re-editing of my old book on 'Work and Wages,' at the date of publication so cordially and favourably received, has proved a far harder task than had been anticipated. I had thought simply to reprint; I have had to a great extent to re-write; and the demand has been too heavy for a worn veteran. I might well have desisted. It had probably been better to commit the matter to a young man, free from other calls, fresh in body and in intellect. I have stuck to the job, inspired chiefly by an undying love for my father, whose qualities and whose memory I revere more and more as the years go by. In so far as his—or, indeed, any—name can survive through the mists which enshroud all things after the lapse of fifty years, I should wish my father to be remembered chiefly as he is represented in the portrait so admirably drawn by his friend and biographer, Sir Arthur Helps. I could wish that the men of the present day could recall my father as I remember him in the years long past, when he invited me, as the greatest pleasure he could give

A 2

to his son, then a mere boy, to accompany him on a visit of inspection to a great railway in construction. I have a living impression of those long walks along a line, on which thousands of workers were busily employed. As the news passed that my father was coming every man left off working, though paid by the piece. They lined the road and gave him a hearty cheer. My father shook hands with every ganger, sub-contractor, and, indeed, every navvy whom he remembered. He called them all by their names—in many cases by their Christian names—and inquired how they were getting on. If they were not making fair earnings, terms of contract were revised. Old undertakings in far-off countries were discussed, and recollections were exchanged.

My father was proud of his navvies, and justly so. There were giants in those days. Well do I remember those gangs of sturdy workers, generally men of the North, in stature not inferior to, in weight exceeding, those noble soldiers of the Household Regiments, of which the nation is so proud, and who, in these later days and under unaccustomed conditions, have well and worthily sustained the never-to-be-forgotten glories of the past.

The exertion to which the navvy is accustomed is too severe for the agricultural labourer, until he has become accustomed to the more arduous occupation. When an agricultural labourer begins to work on a railway, he is disposed to lie down at three o'clock in the afternoon, fatigued and incapable of continuing his efforts. After an interval of twelve months, receiving higher wages, and having better food, he will get into fitter condition to perform his task without difficulty. A large contractor, long associated with my father, once told me that at Macclesfield, in 1847, for excavating an unusually heavy cutting, many men from Lincolnshire were employed, not one of whom was under 5 feet 10½ inches in height. Those who have been long connected with railway construction state that they know many navvies who have attained to a great age.

It is good to remember that the public works executed by my father, as a pioneer contractor in almost every part of the civilised world, have proved a lasting benefit to mankind. Cheap and speedy communication has been provided, and, through all the changes which invention has introduced, the railway continues an indispensable resource of civilisation.

'Work and Wages' was originally published as a sequel and supplement to the biography by Sir Arthur Helps.[1] It gave, in so far as the details could be collected, the rates of wages usually paid

[1] *Life and Labours of Thomas Brassey*, 1805-1870.

in every country in which work was undertaken. Daily rates differed widely. It was an invariable rule to pay by the piece for work done. By this system, carefully carried out under skilful superintendence, the cost differed little, except in the case of sparsely peopled countries. This important result of an unequalled experience in every quarter of the globe was published to the world in 'Work and Wages.' It was shown how rare were the advantages, how common the disadvantages, of cutting down the reward of labour.

The writer has a due sense of the restrictions which should be imposed on whatever might savour of praise of self. It is, however, simple justice to say that the publication of 'Work and Wages,' in 1872, was an incident which, at the time and in the circumstances, seemed, in the words of Mr. and Mrs. Sidney Webb, to mark an epoch. The estimate of enlightened public opinion must be gauged by the criticisms of the Press. They were numerous and in every case commendatory. Nothing can be quoted at this late date beyond one specimen of the language of the reviewers of long ago. 'Work and Wages' was honoured by notices in the 'Quarterly' and the 'Edinburgh.' Having the latter at hand, it may perhaps be permissible to reprint a brief extract :

Work and Wages. By THOMAS BRASSEY, M.P.

London : 1872.

'No subject can more urgently demand, or more amply repay, the study of the intelligent inquirer than the great question of Work. From the inexhaustible fountain of labour springs all that constitutes the wealth of nations. The power, the dignity, and the happiness of a people are at the same time the result, and the expression, of the energy and capacity for labour which characterise the race. From the wheel of the potter, from the yet ruder shed of the brickmoulder, to the noblest work of the sculptor ; from the rudest scratching of the soil to the highest triumph of scientific agriculture ; from the first lesson in the dame school to the master-speech of the great statesman in the senate ; all that can enrich and ennoble a nation is bound together by the golden links of industry. No philosophy can be other than superficial, no statesmanship can be other than barbarous, that is ignorant or negligent of the great natural laws that regulate the application of Labour.

'To the formation of a theory of industrial law worthy the name of Science, the volume before us furnishes a contribution of extraordinary value. Kindly and worthy motives have led to its production. The writer is evidently anxious to show how thoroughly some of those who have of late spoken loudly on the subject of labour are in ignorance of the very elements of the question they have professed to solve. Nor is he less desirous to raise the courage of those who, looking at the disturbances in our industrial system that are chiefly due to artificial causes, despond as to

the future of the country. But it is not so much in
the argument, as in the rich store of industrial facts,
collected from indicated sources, and brought together
in available order, that the value of the book consists.
Such a field for investigation in industrial philosophy
has not before been offered to the world in so com-
pendious a form ; and the value of the facts collected
is enhanced, rather than diminished, by the consideration that no special theory is propounded by the writer.
Thus we have not only ample illustration of the course
and play of industry, in every quarter of the globe ;
but we have the naked facts presented in a natural
light, without even an unconscious effort so to twist or
so to colour them as to make them available for the
establishment of any favourite dogma.'—*Edinburgh
Review*, July 1873.

Many years have elapsed. The unpretending book
referred to above has long since been out of print.
A few friends, fellow-members of the Political
Economy Club, have expressed the wish that some
portions of it should be reprinted, as being useful
for the guidance of all who have to deal with
the management of labour. In complying with a
request which it was highly gratifying to receive,
the author indulges the hope that he is thereby
doing something to add to the store of economic
knowledge.

'Work and Wages' brought its author under
notice. He was sought for, far and wide, to talk
of his father as an employer of labour. The present

volume includes a reprint of a few of the addresses delivered. The complete list, published in 1878, in a volume entitled 'Lectures on the Labour Question,' comprised lectures given at various places on the following subjects :—

1. Labour and Capital. Birkenhead, 1871.
2. The Nine Hours' Movement. Newcastle, 1873.
3. Wages in 1873. Norwich, 1873.
4. Public Elementary Education in the United States. Hastings, 1873.
5. The Duties of the Church in Relation to the Labour Question. Hastings, 1873.
6. Co-operative Production. Halifax, 1874.[1]
7. The South Wales Colliery Strike, 1874.
8. Influences affecting the Price of Labour in England, 1876.
9. On Canada and the United States. Hastings, 1873.
10. Work and Wages in 1877. Leicester, 1877.[1]
11. Labour at Home and Abroad. Leicester, 1877.[1]
12. Comparative Efficiency of English and Foreign Labour. London, 1878.
13. The Rise of Wages in the Building Trades of London. London, 1878.[1]

From a later volume, which appeared in 1879, the chapter on 'Foreign Competition—the Comparative Efficiency of English and Foreign Labour,' is here republished.

It may not unfittingly be added that the task of compilation which the author of 'Work and Wages'

---

[1] Now reprinted.

was originally moved to undertake was one of
extreme difficulty. His honoured father, the first
organiser of labour on the colossal scale required
by modern enterprises of transportation, had left
no record of his work behind, except the faithful
remembrances of his chief employés. Their assistance was invoked. They were severally interviewed,
and invited to record their recollections of service.
Their depositions were taken down by Messrs.
Gurney in shorthand, and formed some twenty-
four volumes of manuscript. From these materials
Sir Arthur Helps compiled his memoir, entitled
'Life and Labours of Thomas Brassey,' and the
present writer the volume on 'Work and Wages.'
For both of us it is enough to say that we sought
no reward. Ours was a labour of love.

                                             B.

December 4, 1915.

CONTENTS

CHAPTER   PAGE

I.   Conditions of Labour 1

II.   Wages and the Cost of Work 8

III.   Wages Generally 27

IV.   Co-operative Production 49

V.   Familistère de Guise 82

VI.   Work and Wages in 1877 88

VII.   Labour at Home and Abroad 103

VIII.   On the Rise of Wages in the Building Trades
of London 115

IX.   Foreign Competition—Comparative Efficiency
of English and Foreign Labour . . . 145

WORK AND WAGES

CHAPTER I

CONDITIONS OF LABOUR

IT seems fitting to open with a few general remarks as to the rights and claims of workers. The present writer thankfully remembers that he was from the beginning able to take an unprejudiced view of the organisation of labour. He never shared the fears of those who thought that Trades Unions had the power to extort rates of payment on a non-remunerative basis from employers of labour.

'When,' says Adam Smith, 'in any country the demand for those who live by wages is continually increasing, the workmen have no occasion to combine to raise their wages. The demand increases necessarily with the increase of the revenue and stock of every country, and cannot possibly increase without it' . . . 'It is in the progressive state, while a society is advancing to further acquisition, rather than when it has acquired its full complement of riches, that the condition of the labouring poor, and of the great body of the people, is the happiest and most comfortable. It is healthy in a stationary, and miserable in a declining state. The progressive state is, in reality, the cheerful and the hearty state

B

in all the different orders of society. The stationary is dull, the declining melancholy.'

After many bitter struggles, the right of combination for the purpose of obtaining improved terms for labour has now been conceded to the working men in every country of the civilised world. There is nothing new under the sun. The Guilds of the Middle Ages were the forerunners of the Trades Unions of to-day. The strikes of modern times have had their counterpart in the Jacquerie riots of the fourteenth century.

When we take into view the great changes brought about in the industrial organisation of this country during the last century—the substitution of steam for manual power, and of machinery for hand labour—and remember that the resources of science can be fully developed only when applied on a large scale, the reasons why workmen have gathered together in recent times, in number so vast, round our great industrial centres, are not far to seek. When operatives have been thus assembled in great numbers, under the same roof, tending the same machine, and working at the same table, is it not natural—nay, reasonable—that they should take combined action on all questions of mutual interest ? In this most legitimate manner Trades Unions have had their origin.

The recognition of the rights of free labour came late in the history of the world. Neither the Greeks nor the Romans recognised the liberty of labour. From the third to the thirteenth century the Church was the most faithful protector of the labouring man. In later times, Parliaments did much to secure liberty for the labourer. Turgot, the First Minister of Louis XVI., fully appreciated the rights of free labour. In his Edict of 1776 he says :— 'Dieu, en donnant à l'homme des besoins, a fait du droit de travailler la propriété de tous les hommes, et cette propriété est la première, la plus sacrée, et la plus imprescriptible de toutes.' This Edict, the first proclamation of the just and equitable principles now universally accepted, was cancelled in the darker times, after the fall of Turgot.

No employer, on any fair view of conditions, can object in principle to the organisation of labour. We cannot but honour and admire the sentiments of fraternal sympathy which prompt men to promote each other's advancement in life by that mutual aid and support which Trades Unions are intended to afford. Trades Unions, like large standing armies, may be a provocation of war ; but if a strike should unfortunately occur the conduct of the workmen will probably be as much superior to that of the rioters in the manufacturing districts in the early part of the present century as the discipline of a standing army is superior to that of a guerilla band.

In the days when ' Work and Wages ' was first printed, Sir Francis Crossley was taking a leading and broadminded part among employers of labour. In a debate on the appointment of the Trades Unions Commission in 1867, he said there was ' a good deal of unreasonable feeling abroad that it was wrong for working men to sell their labour at

the best price. Their labour was the only thing
that they had to sell ; and the best thing to do was
to leave these matters to take their natural course.
It was a great mistake, on the part of employers,
to suppose that the lowest priced labour was always
the cheapest. If there were not so much desire to
run down the price of labour, and the masters showed
a more conciliatory spirit, there would be fewer
strikes and outrages.'

So, too, by Mr. John Stuart Mill ; ' Wages,
like other things, are regulated, either by competition or by custom. In this country there are
few kinds of labour of which the remuneration
would not be lower than it is if the employers took
full advantage of their power.'

The conditions of labour, whether in regard to
profits or in regard to wages, are complex in the
highest degree. Bastiat, in his ' Harmonies Econo-
miques,' said, and said truly : ' Le capital, jusqu'où
qu'il porte ses prétentions, et quelque heureux
qu'il soit dans ses efforts pour les faire triompher,
ne peut jamais placer le travail dans une condition
pire que l'isolement. En d'autres termes, le capital
favorise toujours plus le travail par sa présence
que par son absence.' This is a statement of fact
which all thinkers admit. How unreasonable to
expect ready assent to such a proposition from rude
and untaught workers with the hand.

The energy and the enterprise for which the
leaders of British industry are justly renowned,
while of advantage under prosperous conditions
in increasing the employment of labour, inevitably

lead to fluctuation and trouble. Again and again production has been unduly stimulated in every branch of British industry. When the reaction has taken place and prices have fallen, from the markets being overstocked, we are told that the price of labour and foreign competition are the causes of our inevitable misfortunes. It was well said by an able and candid writer in the *Leeds Mercury*, ' If foreign competition were the cause of our distress, we should be justified in expecting that, in countries competing successfully with us, the manufacturers would be in a prosperous state.' This was not the case. All were calling out at the same time that they were ruined by foreign competition.

At the date of the publication of ' Work and Wages,' the Halifax Chamber of Commerce gave utterance to the well-considered opinion that ' it was demonstrable that the great cause of the depression and the unremunerative character of the worsted trade had been the too rapid increase of machinery, both in spinning and weaving, which were stimulated both by permanent and temporary causes, such as the French Treaty and the American War.'

The same remarks would apply equally to the iron trade and all the other leading industries of the country. The very spirit of enterprise which has made England prosperous tends to produce great fluctuations in the labour market. When trade is good, our ironfounders and cotton-spinners are only too ready to increase the productive resources of their establishments.

In former days wages on the Thames were exceptionally high. In proof of the preference shown by the working classes for a more moderate rate of wage with constant employment, wages in the dockyards may be compared with those paid in private shipbuilding yards. A table was compiled by Admiral King Hall, C.B., giving the rates in Sheerness Yard in the years 1849, 1859, and 1869. Tables showing the current rates at the corresponding period in the private yards on the Thames were prepared by Mr. John Hughes, sometime manager of the Millwall Works. These were published in the first edition of 'Work and Wages.'

At a time when shipwrights in London were earning from 6s. 6d. to 7s. a day, the shipwrights in Sheerness Yard, men at least as skilled as those employed by the private shipbuilders, were content with 4s. 6d. Though they could at any time have put their tools into their baskets, and at the end of an hour and a half's journey by rail have obtained employment from the private shipbuilders at the higher rate of wages, they preferred more moderate wages with a certainty of employment, to higher wages under more precarious conditions.

The rate of wages cannot long continue so high as to deprive capital of its fair return. Neither can it long continue below the amount necessary to maintain the labourer and his family. The fluctuations between the two limits depend entirely upon the varying demand for labour. To the employer, rates of wages are of small importance. The essential is to get the work in hand done for a certain sum of money. The scale of wages should be liberal. It should be fixed. This brings us to the plan, everywhere, in so far as it was practicable, adopted by the writer's father—that of payment by the piece.

Mr. Mault, Secretary to the Builders' Association of Birmingham, stated to the Trades Unions Commissioners that of the 900,000 men employed in the building trades, not more than 90,000 were members of Trades Unions and that, although aiming at securing uniformity throughout the country, the wages of masons varied in different parts from $4\frac{1}{2}d.$ to $7\frac{3}{8}d.$ per hour, the wages of bricklayers from $4\frac{1}{2}d.$ to $8d.$, and those of carpenters from $4\frac{5}{8}d.$ to $8\frac{1}{2}d.$ These figures conclusively prove the fallacy of the idea that Trades Unions can secure for their clients uniform rates of wages.

Organisation may lead to an advance of wages at a somewhat earlier date. Competition among employers would be equally beneficial to the working people. Mr. Robinson, Managing Director of the Atlas Works, Manchester, said in his evidence before the Trades Unions Commissioners : 'I do not think the Unions have altered the rate of wages. The changes are rather due to the demand for labour in particular branches. Between 1851 and 1861 no advance took place in the wages of the engineers, though theirs is the most powerful of the Trades Societies ; in the case of the boiler makers, without the aid of labour organisation wages rose from 26s. to 32s. 6d.'

CHAPTER II

WAGES AND THE COST OF WORK

DAILY wages afford no real measure of the actual cost of work. Let us take examples near home. At the commencement of the construction of the North Devon Railway the wages of the labourers were 2s. a day. During the progress of the work their wages were raised to 2s. 6d. and 3s. a day. The work was executed more cheaply when the men were earning the higher rate of wage than when they were paid at the lower rate. Again, in London, in carrying out a part of the Metropolitan Drainage Works in Oxford Street, the wages of the brick-layers were gradually raised from 6s. to 10s. a day ; the brickwork was constructed at a cheaper rate per cubic yard after the wages of the workmen had been raised to 10s. than when they were paid at the rate of 6s. a day.

On the Grand Trunk Railway a number of French-Canadian labourers were employed. Their wages were 3s. 6d. a day, while the Englishmen received from 5s. to 6s. a day. The English did the greatest amount of work for the money.

The wages of the Dutchmen engaged in the construction of the Dutch Rhenish Railway varied from 1s. 6d. to 1s. 8d. a day, when paid by the day. At piecework they could earn 2s. or 2s. 6d. Good workmen from the Lincolnshire fens would have made 3s. 6d. at similar work.

Both English and French masons were employed in large numbers on the Alderney Breakwater in 1852. The Englishmen earned 5s. 6d. to 6s. ; the Frenchmen 4s. a day.

An opportunity occurred during the building of the refreshment-room at Basingstoke for testing the cost of work with great accuracy. On one side of the station a London bricklayer was employed at 5s. 6d. a day, and on the other two country bricklayers at 3s. 6d. a day. It was found, by measuring the amount of work performed, without the knowledge of the men employed, that the London bricklayer laid, without undue exertion, more bricks in a day than his two less skilful country fellow-labourers.

In the construction of the Paris and Rouen Railway in 1842 an opportunity was afforded of comparing British and foreign wages and cost of work. This Railway was the first large work executed on the Continent. About 10,000 men were employed in its construction, of whom upwards of 4000 were Englishmen. Such an exodus of English labour to continental Europe never before occurred. A special effort was made to secure the services of English workmen on this particular contract. It was a question whether native workmen could be obtained in sufficient numbers, and it was still more doubtful whether they would possess the necessary skill and experience for carrying out railway works, at that period a novelty, even to English engineers, and entirely unknown on the Continent. Under these exceptional circumstances a large body of Englishmen were sent over to Normandy.

The contractors sought by every possible means to mitigate the inconveniences of residence in a foreign country. They established schools and provided clergymen. An English physician was appointed as superior medical attendant for the whole of the works. Resident surgeons attended the sick and wounded, and also the wives of the workmen. It is scarcely necessary to observe that the employment of English manual labour abroad must always be costly, and a somewhat doubtful policy. In this particular case it was not found to be disadvantageous from a pecuniary point of view.

The contract for the Paris and Rouen line included some difficult works. There were four bridges across the Seine, and four tunnels, one of them one mile and five-eighths in length, passing through hard limestone. The English were chiefly employed on the difficult work. The French labourers drew away the stuff, or wound it up the shafts. The mining was done by Englishmen. In the tunnels the skilled work was all carried out by them. At one time there were five hundred Englishmen living in the village of Rollebois, most of whom were employed in the adjacent tunnel. These English navvies earned 5*s.* a day ; the Frenchmen 2*s.* 6*d.* a day. On comparing the cost of two adjacent cuttings in precisely similar circumstances, the excavation was made at a lower cost per cubic yard by the English navvies than by the French labourers.

In the same quarry, at Bonnières, in which Frenchmen, Irishmen, and Englishmen were employed side by side, the Frenchmen received three francs, the Irishmen four, and the Englishmen six francs a day. The Englishman was the most advantageous workman of the three.

It may be gathered from the experience obtained on my father's Continental contracts that, as a general rule, the superiority of English workmen was most conspicuous when they first commenced work in a country in which no railways had been previously constructed. The inexperience of the French in large engineering works is proved conclusively by the fact that the works on the Paris and Rouen line having been divided into innumerable separate contracts, for each of which a separate tender was made, in every case the tender of Messrs. Brassey and Mackenzie was fifty per cent. under the lowest tender of the French contractors. Increased experience enabled the French workmen to earn higher wages, and, on the other hand, closer contact with men of less vigorous habits gradually diminished the energy of the English labourers. For ordinary work, Frenchmen soon become almost as efficient as Englishmen, as the following dialogue with Mr. Milroy, a member of my father's staff, clearly explains :—

'In the particular work you have been speaking of, the two great trades employed were masons and carpenters ? ' Mr. Milroy : ' Yes, I found plenty of

good masons and carpenters in France. The latter
are, in my opinion, superior for such works to
English carpenters, both in the quality of the work
done and in the price at which they do it. Their
tools also are particularly well adapted to the work.
This may arise from Paris having been, in a great
measure, built of timber, filled in between with
small rubble stones and stucco, and then plastered
outside. The men seemed to have acquired a
speciality for that work, and could do it better than
any carpenters I have ever seen. What I have
stated was proved in 1853, when I went back. I
then went on to the Caen and Cherbourg line.
There was only a sprinkling of Englishmen then.
The agents and sub-contractors, who went out with
me, had acquired the language sufficiently, when
formerly engaged in France, to carry on their
communications with the French workmen without
interpreters. Upon the Paris and Rouen line we had
a large proportion of English labourers, but on the
Caen and Cherbourg line a very small proportion ;
yet the one line was constructed quite as cheaply as
the other.'

And now let us turn to leading foreign authorities
on the relative value of English and French labour.
The speeches of M. Thiers and the protectionists
in the French Chamber described the condition of
French industry in years long past in terms which
give little occasion for envious feelings in the English
reader. They say that in mixed woollen and cotton
stuffs England had beaten France ; that we produced 10,000,000 tons of iron as contrasted with an

annual production of 1,000,000 tons in France ; that the French had no heavy goods to export ; that having given up differential rates, they had to import all their colonial and eastern produce from England ; and that the merchant navy was rapidly decaying. Comparing the relative positions of England and France, in reference to cotton manufactures, M. Thiers stated that while England worked up 3,000,000, France only worked up from 600,000 to 700,000 bales, and that the cost of production was from 15 to 20 per cent. less in England than in France. 'It was,' he said, 'the cheap industry of Rouen which suffered most from English competition. The genius of England was for cheapness —that of France for quality.'

The relative importance of the cotton manufacture in the different countries of Europe was also compared by M. de Forcade in the course of the same debate. His statement gave the following results : that England had 30,000,000 spindles, France 6,800,000, the Zollverein 2,500,000, Russia 1,800,000, Austria 1,700,000, Switzerland 1,500,000, Belgium 600,000, and Italy 450,000 spindles. It is well here to remind the reader that the statistics quoted represent the state of things fifty years ago.

As in these later days so in earlier times costs of work have been reduced by improved methods, and by the greatly extended use of machines.

Mr. Nasmyth, in his evidence before the Trades Unions Commissioners, described how the long strike of 1851 developed to the utmost the use of labour-saving machinery. 'The great feature,' he said, 'of our modern mechanical improvement has been the introduction of self-acting tools. All that a mechanic has to do, and which any lad is able to do, is, not to labour, but to watch the beautiful functions of the machine. All that class of men who depended upon mere dexterity are set aside altogether. I had four boys to one mechanic. By these mechanical contrivances I reduced the number of men in my employ, 1500 hands, fully one half. The result was that my profits were much increased.'

'In the cotton mill of Messrs. Houldsworths, in Glasgow, a spinner employed on a mule of 3360 spindles and spinning cotton 120 hanks to the pound, produced, in 1823, working 74½ hours in the week, 46 pounds of yarn, his nett weekly earnings for which amounted to 26s. 7d. In 1833, the rate of wages having in the meanwhile been reduced 13⅓ per cent., and the time of working having been lessened to 69 hours, the spinner was enabled by the greater perfection of the machinery to produce, on a mule of the same number of spindles, 52½ pounds of yarn of the same fineness, and his nett weekly earnings were advanced to 29s. 10d.'

A much more considerable economy than this was effected by increasing the size of the mules. Mr. Cowell, in the Supplementary Report of the Factory Commissioners, gave the following example of the effect on the spinner's earnings :—' In the early part of last year a spinner produced 16 pounds of yarn of No. 200 from mules of the power of 300 to 324 spindles. Consulting the list of prices, I perceive

that in May he was paid 3*s*. 6*d*. a pound ; this gives
54*s*. for his gross receipts, out of which he had to
pay 13*s*. for assistants. This leaves him with 41*s*.
earnings. His mules are now converted into mules
of the power of 648 ; he is paid 2*s*. 5*d*. a pound
instead of 3*s*. 6*d*. ; but he produces 32 pounds of
yarn of the fineness of 200 hanks to the pound in
69 hours. His gross receipts are immediately raised
to 77*s*. 4*d*. He requires five assistants to help him ;
but deducting 27*s*. for their pay from his gross
receipts, there remains a sum of 50*s*. 4*d*. for his net
earnings for 69 hours' work, instead of 41*s*., an
increase of more than 20 per cent., while the cost
of the yarn is reduced 13*d*. per pound.'

Mr. Alfred Field describing, as must often be
repeated, the state of things fifty years ago, told the
Committee on Scientific Education that, in the
United States, a workman in the hardware trade
earned double the daily wages of an English workman ; but labour-saving appliances had been
brought to such perfection that in twenty-five classes
of hardware goods the United States were able to
export largely into countries in which the pay of
artisans is scarcely a quarter of the wage paid in
America. They sent their spades, shovels, axes,
coopers' tools, and pumps to England ; although
raw material and wages were twice as dear in the
United States as in England.

It is by improved methods of husbandry and
by superior machinery alone that agriculturists are
enabled to pay higher wages and higher rents and
yet obtain a moderate return on their capital, and

some remuneration for their scientific education and personal attention to their business.

As an instance of the incapacity of unskilled men in its most exaggerated form, I may mention a case which occurred in Jamaica, on the only railway which had been executed in that Island. The usual plant required for the construction of the railway had been sent out, and the native labourers were supplied with barrows for the purpose of removing the earth. When these men began to work they were so ignorant of the mechanical advantages to be derived from the use of the barrow that they placed these vehicles, laden with earth, upon the top of their heads ; and it was not without much expostulation that the English foremen were enabled to induce them to try the effect of placing the barrow on a plank, and wheeling instead of carrying the load.

A few remarks may now be offered, showing, in numerous instances, that low rates of wages by no means ensure low cost of work. The examples quoted are taken mainly from official reports from Russia, Eastern Europe, Belgium, America, India. First let us take a report by Mr. Michell as to economic conditions in Russia at the date when he wrote.

An apprehension of the military power of Russia, which a certain school of politicians are too ready to entertain, might, perhaps, be changed to pity if they knew the condition of the Russian peasantry, and their inability to bear the strain of a long protracted war. Even in peace they were engaged throughout their lives in an exhausting struggle for bare existence. From abject poverty the women were compelled to share unceasingly in the out-door labours of the men. The infant mortality in Russia in years gone by was appalling. The peasant women of Russia gave birth to their off-spring under circumstances equally perilous to the life of the mother and the child. Their confinement often took place in a barn or a stable. They had no medical attendance, and in three days at the utmost they were once more employed in hard field labour. The result of such privation and suffering was that a large proportion of infants died within a week after their birth. The number of males living at the age of five years, in proportion to the total number of the population, was $20\frac{3}{4}$ per cent. less in Russia than in Great Britain, France, and Belgium. The shortness of the average duration of life in Russia was equally lamentable. In the North-West Pro-vinces, the average limit of life was between twenty-two and twenty-seven. In the Volga basin and South-Eastern Provinces it was twenty years ; in Viatka, Perm, and Orenburg, only fifteen years.

The Blue Book on the Tenure of Land in Foreign Countries did honour to our diplomatic service. Numerous examples were given, showing that where labour is cheapest, the indifference to labour-saving machinery was most conspicuous ; and that where labour was dearest it was most effectually economised. These axioms were strikingly illus-trated by a comparison of the agriculture of Russia and Prussia with the agriculture of the United States and of those European countries in which labour was most liberally paid.

In Russia the day labourer's wages ranged from
8*d*. to 1*s*. 4*d*. with food, the cost of which was from
2*d*. to 3*d*. a day. The average pay of the female
labourer was 6½*d*. a day, with the addition of food.
During harvest, the male labourer could command
from 1*s*. 4*d*. to 2*s*. 8*d*. a day with food ; the female
labourer from 9½*d*. to 2*s*. 8*d*. a day with food. The
yield of crops in Russia was said by Mr. Michell to
be less than half the yield obtained in England or
Saxony, and smaller than in any other country in
Europe.

The miserable pay of the women employed in the
manufactories of Russia suggests some observations
as to the evils which necessarily arise from sub-
jecting the female population to excessive manual
labour. In all the less civilised countries of Europe
women are compelled to share in the manual labours
of men. This practice is in a large degree the cause
of that very poverty which it is intended to alleviate.
The introduction of so many additional hands into
the labour market has a marked effect in diminishing
the reward of labour. On the Lemberg-Czernowitz
line, in some places, half the people employed were
women. They earned 1.60 franc a day, and the men
from 2 to 3 francs a day.

Mr. Mill in his ' Political Economy ' quotes a
statement by Professor Jones, in which he said that
the Russians, or rather those German writers who
have observed the manners and habits of Russia,
supply some remarkable facts : ' Two Middlesex
mowers,' they say, ' will mow in a day as much grass
as six Russian serfs, and in spite of the dearness of

provisions in England and their cheapness in Russia, the mowing of a quantity of hay, which would cost the English farmer half a copeck, will cost the Russian proprietor three or four copecks.' The Prussian Councillor of State, Jacobi, is considered to have proved that in Russia, where everything is cheap, the labour of the serf was twice as expensive as that of the labourer in England. In Austria the labour of a serf was one-third of that of a free hired labourer.

Let us turn from Russia to Eastern Europe. On the Bukovina line the wages of the men for picking were 1s. 6d. per day, while the women, who worked only with the shovel, earned about 6d. a day less than the men. The cost of living for a man and his wife and three children in Hungary may be stated approximately at 1s. a day. In those countries the cost of unskilled labour is small. The struggle for life is so severe that every child, the moment it can add the smallest fraction to the earnings of the family, is sent into the fields. The sacrifice of these earnings, however scanty, for a few years, for the purpose of acquiring a knowledge of a skilled trade, is impossible with a peasantry so destitute. The cost of skilled labour is thus disproportionately high.

Speaking of Ireland—the Ireland of over half a century ago—Mr. Joseph Hume, in a speech on the Combination Laws, delivered in the House of Commons on June 29, 1825, said that he had heard it stated 'that low wages were a good thing. That he denied. Low wages tended to degrade the labourer.

It was the high wages which the English artisan received, compared with the miserable pay of the Irish labourer, which made the former so superior in energy.'

The inferiority of the Irish labourer in the days of Mr. Hume is described and fully explained in the Report of the Irish Railways Commissioners presented to Parliament in 1837 : ' In the northern province the people were better lodged, clothed, and fed than in the other provinces ; wages were higher. Food consisted chiefly of meal, potatoes, and milk.'

' In the southern districts the food of the population was inferior, consisting at best of potatoes and milk, without meal. The wage of the labourer varied from 1s. to 8d. a day. The condition of the inhabitants of the western district was inferior even to that of the people of the south of Ireland. Their food consisted of potatoes alone, without meal, and, in most cases, without milk. Their cabins were wretched hovels, their beds were of straw, and the wages of the labourer were reduced to the lowest point, being, upon the average, not more than 6d. a day.' Poverty and misery had deprived the people of all energy. Every motive to exertion was destroyed ; agriculture was in the rudest and the lowest state.

The effect of these depressing circumstances, aggravated of course by the backward state of agriculture, was strikingly illustrated in the deficiency of produce, and in the amount of work performed by Irish labour, compared with that of the same class in England.

The Irish Poor Law Commissioners stated that the average produce of the soil in Ireland was not much above one half the average produce in England, whilst the number of labourers employed in agriculture was, in proportion to the quantity of land under cultivation, more than double, viz. as five to two. Thus ten labourers in Ireland raised only the same quantity of produce that four labourers raised in England, and this produce was generally of an inferior quality. So striking a disproportion, though generally admitting of very considerable qualification with reference to the different nature and degree of facilities afforded to the labourer in the two countries, still showed a decided advantage in favour of the English workman, and went far to prove the dearness of ill-requited labour.

Turn to India. On the Delhi and Umritzar Railway it was found, as I was informed by Mr. Henfrey, my father's resident partner, that, mile for mile, the cost of railway work was about the same as in England. Earthwork was executed by the coolies at a cheaper rate than at home, but native skilled labour was more expensive. The wages paid were :—masons, 10 to 12 rupees a month ; carpenters, 15 to 18 ; bricklayers, 8 to 12. The execution of the works on a railway in India was generally undertaken by small contractors or middlemen, who in many cases were shopkeepers. There was a difficulty in obtaining experienced sub-contractors, and in consequence it was necessary to employ a numerous body of English foremen. Hence the cost of supervision was greatly enhanced,

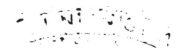

and was found to amount on the average to twenty per cent. on the entire outlay.

Before the railways caused an increased demand for labour in India, wages ranged from 4*d*. to 4½*d*. a day. The demand for labour raised wages considerably. Even then the coolies were not paid more than 6*d*. a day. These wages far more than sufficed to supply their wants. Their food consisted of two pounds of rice a day, mixed with a little curry. The cost of living on this, their usual diet, was only 1*s*. a week. For 1*s*. 6*d*. they could live in comparative luxury. On the railways of India it has been found that great increase of pay has neither augmented the rapidity of execution nor added to the comfort of the labourer. The Hindoo workman knows no other want than his daily portion of rice. The torrid climate renders water-tight habitations and ample clothing alike unnecessary. The labourer therefore desists from work as soon as he has provided for the necessities of the day. Higher pay adds nothing to his comforts ; it serves but to diminish his ordinary industry.

In proportion as skill and manual dexterity are required, the differences in the cost of constructing engineering works disappear. In Italy, as in India, it has been found that a numerous but unskilled population, in a climate where the necessaries of life are inexpensive, can undertake the mere manual labour at a cheaper rate than in England ; though this is only true when works are not pushed on so rapidly as to require the importation of labour from a distance. When the local labourers are alone employed, the Italian villagers, men, women, and children, carrying earth to and fro in baskets on their heads, and as ignorant as the coolies themselves of the resources and appliances of mechanical science, can execute earthwork about as cheaply as in India. On the other hand, masonry and other work requiring skilled labour is rather dearer in Italy than in England.

In Mauritius the interesting experience acquired in the construction of a railway by my father's partner, Mr. Longridge, established the same result as in the cases already quoted. Though the daily wages were low, with due allowance for extra supervision, the cost of earthwork, rock cutting, and masonry was quite as great as the cost in England. Skilled work, as, for example, carpentry, was from twenty to twenty-five per cent. more costly in Mauritius than in England.

The wages paid in Great Britain are higher than in any other country Yet even with respect to bridges, viaducts, tunnels, and all works of art on railways, they can be executed at a cheaper rate in England than in any other country in the world, where the rate of wages is lower. Masonry costs as much in Italy as in Manchester. This approximate uniformity of cost is exhibited in all cases. The superiority of the Englishman to the workman of other nations was equally remarkable, whenever there was an opportunity of employing them side by side.

The differences of character and capabilities, which tend in such a remarkable degree to establish an equality in the cost of labour in every part of the world, have occupied the attention of many thoughtful and penetrating minds. Mr. John Stuart Mill says that 'individuals or nations do not differ so much in the efforts they are able and willing to make under strong immediate incentives, as in their capacity of present exertion for a distant object, and in the thoroughness of their application to work on ordinary occasions. This last quality is the principal industrial excellence of the English people. This efficiency of labour is connected with their whole character, with their defects as much as with their good qualities. The majority of Englishmen have no life but in their work—that alone stands between them and ennui. The absence of any taste for amusement or enjoyment of repose is common to all classes. The effect is that where hard labour is the thing required, there are no better labourers than the English.'

The experience of practical men confirms the opinion expressed by Montesquieu, in the 'Esprit des Lois'—'Il y a dans l'Europe une espèce de balancement entre les nations du Midi et celles du Nord. Les premières ont toute sorte de commodités pour la vie et pour les besoins ; les secondes ont beaucoup de besoins et peu de commodités pour la vie. L'équilibre se maintient par la paresse qu'elle a donnée aux nations du Midi, et par l'industrie et l'activité qu'elle a données à celles du Nord.'

In a paper furnished to the Select Committee on East India Finance by Sir Bartle Frere, some remarkable examples were given of a rise in wages in consequence of the increased competition for labour for railways and other great public works. The following table shows the variations in the average monthly wages of a carpenter in Bombay :

1830–39	1840–49	1850–59	1863
s. d.	s. d.	s. d.	s.
30 4	28 10	32 7½	58

The wages of a coolie at the same periods were :

1830–39	1840–49	1850–59	1863
s. d.	s. d.	s. d.	s. d.
14 9½	12 3½	14 2	27 0

Everywhere in the vicinity of railway works the Collectors remark on their great effect in raising wages. The practice of promptly paying for all labour in liberal money-wages caused an important social revolution in the habits of all who live by labour, even at a great distance from the railway works. The labourers often travelled from their homes 200 miles to obtain work so paid, returning home at the harvest-time.

The rise in wages in Bombay had increased the number of consumers of superior qualities of grain and meat. The increased consumption had raised the cost of living. The advance in the cost of living had had the effect of raising the rate of wages. Moreover, the increased external trade of Bombay, the influx of money for the purchase of commodities and the consequent depreciation in the purchasing power of bullion, and the increased demand for labour, had by their combined influence produced an astonishing advance of wages in Bombay, as compared with Bengal.

The difference between the rates in Bengal and Bombay is shown below :

	In Bengal per Month Rupees	In Bombay per Month Rupees
Carpenters	9	25
Masons	$5\frac{5}{16}$	21
Labouring coolies . . .	6	$9\frac{10}{16}$
Horse-keepers . . .	5	$8\frac{9}{16}$

I quote the following from Mr. Michell · 'It is fortunate that such an amelioration of the condition of the people is taking place. In many districts black bread and water are the only food of the people, and the cost of this meagre dietary varies from 5s. to 6s. a month.

'Since 1853 we have subscribed no less than £40,000,000 for Indian Railways. A considerable portion of this sum has been paid to native labourers, and the result has been that in the districts traversed by these railways wages have advanced within a short time no less than 100 per cent. In consequence of the great demand for workmen, the price of labour has increased to an extent still more marvellous in Bombay.'

CHAPTER III

In the widely scattered countries over which my father's labours extended fluctuations in the rates, as might have been expected, were wide. Let us first take the wages current at the period when my father first engaged in the construction of railways.

In the year 1837, on the Penkridge viaduct of the Grand Junction Railway, wages for navvies were 2s. 6d. to 2s. 8d. per day, artisans 22s. to 23s. per week. On the works of the Aire and Calder Navigation, executed in 1836, navvies working in butty-gangs by piecework earned from 4s. to 5s., and in some cases 6s. per day. On the London and Birmingham Railway plate-layers, working on the piece-work system, earned, by the day, 3s. 6d.

In 1837 wages advanced in Manchester from 4s. to 4s. 6d. per day. Working hours—on Monday from 7 a.m. to 6 p.m.; on the four following days 6 a.m. to 6 p.m.; on Saturday 6 a.m. to 4 p.m. An hour and three quarters each day was allowed for meals. Thus the earnings were £1 7s. for 59½ hours of work. (In the spring of 1869 the wages in Manchester were £1 13s. for a week of 55 hours.)

On the Trent Valley line, completed in 1846, wages of navvies averaged 3s. to 3s. 6d. On many portions of the contract, during a great part of the time in which it was being executed, the men worked night and day. At Nuneaton there was no difficulty in engaging 100 men in the course of three days to be employed in night work alone. Men could not be found to do night work so readily at the present time.

The following statement, prepared by Mr. Mackay, a fine fellow whom I well remember as for many years in the employ of my father, gives the weekly wages earned by men employed on railway works from 1843 to 1869. The notes furnish a comparative statement of the cost of work represented by the different rates of wages, and contain a short explanation of the extent of the demand for labour at the different periods included in the Return :—

PERIODS.

	1843	1846	1849	1851	1855	1857	1860	1863	1866	1869
	s. d.	s. d.	s. d.	s. d.	s. d.	s. d.	s. d.	s. d.	s. d.	s. d.
Masons . .	21 0	33 0	24 0	21 0	25 6	24 0	22 6	24 0	27 0	27 0
Bricklayers .	21 0	30 0	24 0	21 0	25 6	22 6	22 6	24 0	27 0	25 6
Carpenters and Blacksmiths .	21 0	30 0	22 6	21 0	24 0	22 6	22 6	24 0	25 6	24 0
Navvies, Getters (Pickmen) .	16 6	24 0	18 0	15 0	19 0	18 0	17 0	19 0	20 0	18 0
Navvies, Fitters (Shovellers) .	15 0	22 6	16 6	14 0	17 0	17 0	16 0	17 0	18 0	17 0
Cost of labour only, per cube yard :										
Of brickwork .	2 3	3 9	2 9	2 3	2 6	2 6	2 4	2 6	2 9	2 6
Of earthwork .	0 4½	0 7½	0 5	0 4	0 5½	0 5½	0 5	0 5½	0 5¾	0 5½

1843.   'Gloucester and Bristol Railway, period of general depression, provisions for men and horses very cheap. Men plentiful, excellent workmen. Clay cuttings, on the Gloucester to Stonehouse line, taken out at 6d. a yard, inclusive of horse labour.'

1846.   'Lancaster and Carlisle, Caledonian, Trent Valley, North Staffordshire, Eastern Union Railways in construction. Height of the railway mania. Demand for labour much in excess of supply. Work going on night and day, even the same men working continuously for several days and nights. Instances recorded of men being paid for forty-seven days in one lunar month. Provisions dear. Excessively high wages, excessive work, excessive drinking, indifferent lodgings caused great demoralisation to the good old navvy, already on the decline.'

'Great Northern, Oxford, Worcester and Wolverhampton, Oxford and Birmingham, Chester and Holyhead Railways in construction. Great reduction in wages caused by the financial embarrassments in October 1847, and political turmoils and revolutions in 1848 on the Continent and at home. General distrust, aggravated by the unsettled state of affairs abroad. Works stopped in 1847 partially resumed in 1848. The 1846 contracts not yet completed. In 1849 work comparatively plentiful. Provisions moderate in price.' **1849.**

'Shrewsbury and Hereford, North Devon, in construction. Contracts taken in 1846 not all completed. Great depression in the labour market. But little work going on. Political affairs on the Continent unsettled. Provisions very cheap.' **1851.**

'Leicester and Hitchin, Leominster and Kingston Railways in construction. Work still slack during this period. Best men gone to France, Spain, Belgium, Switzerland, and Italy to Mr. Brassey's works. Provisions dear, horse provender excessively high, costing 5s. a day each horse.' **1855.**

1857.   'Shrewsbury and Crewe, Leominster and Kingston Railways in construction. Work still very slack ; the effects of the Crimean War had not wholly passed away.'

1860.   'Knighton and Craven arms, Woofferton and Tenbury, widening of Shrewsbury and Hereford, Severn Valley Railway Works in construction. Men plentiful, provisions cheap.'

1863.   'Tenbury and Bewdley, South Staffordshire, Ludlow and Clee Hill, Wenlock, Nantwich and Drayton, widening of Shrewsbury and Hereford, Worm Valley drainage, Letton Valley drainage in construction. Men plentiful, provisions rather dear.'

1866.   'Wellington and Drayton, widening of Nantwich and Drayton, Hereford Loop, Hooton and Parkgate, Wenlock and Craven arms, Ebbw Vale in construction.'

'Silverdale and Drayton, Sirhowy, widening of Abergavenny and Merthyr Railways, and London drainage works in construction. Provisions rather dear.'

The explanatory memorandum does not exhaust the list of Mr. Brassey's contracts in progress at the several dates mentioned. Those only are included which happened to be in the recollection of the writer, whose immediate field of observation was necessarily limited to a few in the Midland Counties.

The Crimean War produced a marked effect on the rate of wages in every trade, both in England and on the Continent. In the construction of the

Bellegarde Tunnel, two and a half miles in length, on the Lyons and Geneva Railway, the wages of the Piedmontese quarrymen rose from $2\frac{1}{2}$ to 3, $3\frac{1}{2}$, and 4 francs a day. The Englishmen, working in shifts of from six to ten hours each, were paid at the rate of from 8 to 10 francs a day. Their wages were raised, partly on account of the difficult nature of the works. The shafts were from 600 to 700 feet deep.

The same causes were producing the same results on the Continent as in England. In Brussels such was the demand for labour for excavation that the men employed as navvies were actually receiving higher wages than skilled masons. The wages of the navvy in Brussels were 60 centimes an hour, whereas the masons were receiving only 50 centimes.

Turning to the trades not directly connected with railway construction, a review in the columns of the *Economist* furnished a striking illustration of the rise of wages consequent upon the activity of trade.

In 1871 wages rose in the iron, engineering, coal, and hardware trades from fifteen to twenty per cent. In the Cleveland iron trade the rise was even greater. The wages of labourers advanced from 3s. to 4s. a day ; puddlers from 40s. per week to 55s. ; and from 5s. 3d. to 7s. per score of $7\frac{1}{2}$ tons.

In Lancashire and Yorkshire lads were being imported from the country into the cotton trade. Their wages commenced at from 15s. to 16s. per week. The exports from the United Kingdom reached the value of £319,000,000. The greatest increase took place in those trades in which the wages had advanced the most.

Our exports of iron and steel doubled within a period of seven years. The activity of the Welsh iron manufacture was unprecedented. The following statement, prepared by the proprietors of large iron works in South Wales, shows the comparative earnings of the workmen in their employ in the years 1842, 1851, and 1869 :

COMPARATIVE EARNINGS OF WORKPEOPLE EMPLOYED IN IRON MANUFACTURE

Occupation	1842 Price per ton	1842 Wages per week	1851 Price per ton	1851 Wages per week	1869 Price per ton	1869 Wages per week
	s. d.	*s. d.*	*s. d.*	*s. d.*	*s. d.*	*s. d.*
Miners	—	10 0 to 16 0	—	11 0 to 16 0	—	12 0 to 18 0
Colliers	—	14 0 – 16 0	—	15 0 – 18 0	—	16 0 – 20 0
Furnaces:—						
Founders	0 4	17 0 – 18 0	0 3	25 0 – 29 0	$1\frac{6}{10}$	27 0 – 30 0
Fillers	0 4	17 0 – 18 0	0 3	25 0 – 29 0	$1\frac{6}{10}$	27 0 – 30 0
Cinder fillers	0 3¼	15 0 – 16 0	0 2¼	21 0 – 24 0	$1\frac{2}{10}$	20 0 – 22 6
Labourers	—	10 6	—	10 6	—	11 6 – 12 6
Forge:—						
Puddlers	Pig iron nil. Metal, 5 6 1st hand	Share. 16 0 – 16 6 ; 21 0 – 22 0	Pig iron, 4 10 Metal nil 1st hand	Share. 16 0 – 18 0 ; 22 0 – 25 0	4 11 and 5 11 ; 4 0 1st hand	Share. 18 0 – 24 0 ; 28 0 – 32 0
Labourers	—	10 6	—	10 6	—	10 6 – 13 0
Girls	nil		—	4 9	—	5 6 – 6 6
Mills:—						
Heaters	Bar iron 1 5	24 0 – 26 0	Rails 1st heater, 1 1 ; 2nd heater, 6½ ; 0 10¼	25 0 – 27 0 ; 35 0 – 37 0	Rails 1st heater, 10½ ; 2nd heater, 5¼ ; 0 7¾	25 0 – 28 6 ; 35 0 – 40 0
Rollers, &c.	1 8¼ contract	—	—	—	Roller 50 0 ; Rougher 40 0 each	
Labourers	—	10 6	—	10 6	—	11 0 – 12 6
Girls	—	4 9	—	4 9	—	5 6 – 8 0
Carpenters	—	12 6	—	13 0 – 14 0	—	13 0 – 16 6
Pattern Makers	—	13 0 – 14 0	—	13 0	—	13 6 - 19 0
Fitters	—	12 0 – 14 0	—	12 0 – 14 0	—	13 0 – 19 0
Blacksmiths	—	12 0 – 15 6	—	Contract	—	14 0 – 22 6
Masons	—	12 0 – 15 0	—	15 0	—	14 0 – 20 0

D

Take the Continent of Europe. At the great zinc works known as the Vieille Montagne, near Liège, where 6500 hands were employed, in twelve years the wages had increased 45 per cent.

In the famous engine-building establishment at Creuzot, founded by the father of Mr. Charles Manby, 10,000 persons were employed at the period under review. The annual expenditure in wages amounted to £400,000. Mechanics were paid, when the establishment was first created, at the rate of 2½ francs a day. Later on none received less than 5 francs a day. Between 1850 and 1866 the mean rate advanced from 2s. to 2s. 11d. per head, or 38 per cent., and some men earned from 6s. 8d. to 8s. 4d. per day. In addition to their money wages, great facilities were given to the workpeople, at the expense of the proprietors, for feeding, clothing, and educating themselves and their families. Seven hundred families of the operatives were lodged by the company at 50 per cent. below the normal rate of house rent, and 700 gardens were let at the nominal rent of 2 francs per annum.

At MM. Schneider's, without the assistance of a Trades Union, the working people had obtained, during seventeen years, an augmentation of wage of 38 per cent. In England, in the corresponding period, the most powerful of all the Trade Societies, with an accumulated fund of £149,000, had found it impossible to secure any increase in the earnings of its members.

Mr. Fane says, in his report to Lord Stanley, published at the date of publication of 'Work and

Wages' in 1872, that 'the general rate of money wages in France had increased about 40 per cent. in the last fifteen years, in those industries which competed with foreigners in the neutral markets. This rise in the money wages had been accompanied by a considerable rise in the price of food and clothing; still, the relative proportions in which money wages and the price of commodities had risen left a margin in favour of the former.'

Examples without number might be quoted of the rise in wages which contractors had to meet in the execution of works in sparsely peopled countries.

When the Grand Trunk Railway was being constructed in Canada men were engaged in Lancashire and Cheshire. On landing in Canada they received 40 per cent. more than they had been previously earning in England for doing the same work. The cost of the works was about 30 per cent. dearer. The wages of labourers were 3s. 6d. a day at the commencement of the works. They rose to 6s. a day ere they were completed. Masons, whose wages when in England were 5s. a day, and who were taken out to Canada at the expense of the contractors, earned 7s. 6d. a day in the colony; although the cost of living was not greater in Canada than in England. The supply of their labour in England was abundant, while in Canada skilled artisans were comparatively rare.

For the construction of a railway in New South Wales, two thousand men were sent out from England, at the joint expense of the contractors and the Government. The cost of living for a single navvy was 10*s*. a week ; as compared with 8*s*. a week in England. Navvies, who in England had been paid from 3*s*. 3*d*. to 3*s*. 6*d*. per day, received from 7*s*. 6*d*. to 8*s*. ; and the wages of skilled hands were increased in proportion. The daily wages of masons ranged from 11*s*. to 13*s*. ; bricklayers, 11*s*. to 12*s*. ; brickmakers, 8*s*. to 10*s*. ; and carpenters, 10*s*. to 12*s*. ; such an advance in the rate of pay of the same men can only be explained by the altered relations between the supply of labour and the demand in the colony, as contrasted with the mother country.

In Spain, in the construction of the railway from Bilbao to Tudela, the wages earned by labourers, which at the commencement of the contract were 1*s*. a day, rose, before the works were completed, to 3*s*. a day. On the same contract the wages of the masons increased, in the corresponding period, from 1*s*. 4*d*. to 5*s*. a day.

So in other parts of the world. One of the last investigations made on my father's behalf was connected with a project for a complete system of railways in Persia. If the scheme had been carried out, it was assumed that the pay of engine-drivers, fitters, and stationmasters would be £250 a year, and of foremen platelayers £120 a year.

Take South America. A fitter, whose wages in England would be 30*s*. a week, commanded a salary of £200 a year at Rosario in the Argentine Republic. In Lima, in 1869, machinists received 10*s*. 6*d*. to 18*s*. per day ; boilermakers and smiths, 12*s*. to 18*s*. a day ; plumbers, 10*s*. 6*d*. to 15*s*. ; common labourers,

3s. 9d. to 6s. Single men could board at Lima for from 2s. 3d. to 3s. a day, and the rent of houses, containing two or three rooms and a kitchen, varied from £2 5s. to £3 15s. a month.

In Syria the rates of wages were higher than might have been expected—not indeed because capital was abundant, but because the supply of labour was limited. In Alexandretta the daily wages of common labourers were 1s. 4d. ; masons and carpenters were paid from 2s. 7d. to 3s. 7d. a day. In Aleppo the daily wages of masons were 2s. 3d. to 2s. 9d. ; carpenters, 2s. 2d. to 2s. 7d. ; masons' labourers, 1s. 10d., and masons' boys, 1s. 3d.

Miners worked, at the date of the writing of 'Work and Wages,' on the average twelve hours a day in South Wales, seven hours in the North of England. The late Sir George Elliott, M.P., had found that the cost of getting coals in Aberdare was 25 per cent. more than in Northumberland.

Mining and Engine-building.

The interesting publications of Mr. Lowthian Bell, a report to Congress of Mr. Commissioner Wells, the Special Commissioner of Revenue in the United States in 1868, and a report of Mr. Redgrave, one of the Inspectors of Factories, contained many other equally remarkable cases in various trades, all tending to prove that the cost of labour cannot be conclusively determined by the rate of daily wages in the respective industries.

Mr. Lowthian Bell, in an address read at a meeting of ironmasters in the North of England, gave the result of his investigations into the cost of smelting pig-iron in France. By a careful inquiry at a large establishment he had ascertained that forty-two men were there employed to carry out the same amount of work which twenty-five men were able to do at the Clarence factories on the Tees. In spite of the actual labour on a ton of pig-iron for smelting being 20 per cent. cheaper in France than in England, the entire smelting charges were sensibly greater in France than in the general run of work at Middlesbrough. Taking into account the saving in respect of fuel, the cost of producing pig-iron in France was 20s., in some cases even 30s., per ton more than that exhibited by the cost-sheets of the manufacturers.

The average cost of raising coal at the pit's mouth in France was said by Mr. Lowthian Bell to be from 5s. 6d. to 6s. a ton, and the average price of coal 11s. per ton—the price for small coal used by the ironmasters being 8s. 6d. as compared with 5s., the price paid by the Cleveland smelters.

Belgium raised 11,000,000 tons of coal annually, and exported 4,000,000 to France. The average cost of coal at the pit's mouth was from 5s. 6d. to 7s. a ton. The price varied in 1867 from 9s. 6d. to 10s. 6d. a ton. Neither in France nor in Belgium was the cost of extracting the coal reduced by the low price of labour. In the manufacture of iron the opinion of Mr. Bell was confirmed by Mr. Hewett, an American ironmaster, who told the Trades Unions Commissioners that the price of iron was £1 sterling per ton higher at Creuzot than in England, and by M. Michel Chevalier, who, in his introduction to the

Reports of the Jurors of the French Exhibition in 1867, said that rails were from 25 to 30 francs dearer per ton in France than in England. A similar difference was shown in the rails purchased for the Mont Cenis Railway, the price of which at the works in France was from £7 12s. to £8 per ton, while the price in England was £7 per ton. The duty of £2 8s. per ton which was then payable on rails imported into France was a proof of the conscious inability of the French ironmasters to compete with our manufacturers in an open market.

Mr. Commissioner Wells, in a report to the American Congress, discussed in minute detail the comparative cost of labour in the principal manufacturing countries. Taking the puddling of iron as the representative process of the iron trade, he said that he found that the average price of labour per day for puddlers was from 7s. 6d. to 7s. 10d. in Staffordshire ; 6s. 4d. in France ; and from 4s. 9d. to 5s. in Belgium ; yet the average price of merchant bar-iron was £6 10s. in England, £7 in Belgium, and £8 in France.

In a report on the condition of the textile industries in England, Mr. Redgrave, one of Her Majesty's Inspectors of Factories, said that, while the foreigner was under the same conditions as to the raw material as the English manufacturer, and his fuel was more expensive, his workpeople did not work with the same vigour and steadiness as Englishmen. ' All the evidence that has come before me has gone to prove that there is a great preponderance in favour of this country. Comparing the work of a British with a foreign spinner, the average number of persons employed to spindles was—in France, one person to fourteen spindles; in Russia, one to twenty-eight spindles; in Prussia, one to thirty-seven; in Great Britain, one to seventy-four. But I could find many cotton-spinning factories in my district in which mules containing 2200 spindles are managed by one minder and two assistants.' ' I have recently been told,' he continued, ' by one who had been an English manager in a factory at Oldenburg, that though the hours of work were from 5.30 a.m. to 8 p.m. every day, only about the same weight of work was turned off under English overlookers as would be produced in a working day from 6 a.m. to 6 p.m. in this country. Under German overlookers the produce was much less. The wages were 50 per cent. less in many cases than in England. The number of hands, in proportion to machinery, was much larger. In some departments it was in the proportion of five to three. In Russia the inefficiency of the labour of the foreign, as compared with that of the English, operatives was even more striking. On a comparison of the wages, supposing the Russian operatives to work only sixty hours a week as they did in England, instead of seventy-five as in Russia, their wages would not be one-fourth the amount earned in England. The wage must be taken into account with the power of the operative as a producer ; and herein will be found an advantage of the English operative over the foreign competitor sufficient, with some qualification, to counterbalance the mere cheapness of wage.'

Mr. Wells, in the report to which I have already referred, confirmed the view expressed by Mr. Redgrave. He said that, 'whereas female labour in the cotton manufacture was paid at from 12s. to 15s. a week in Great Britain ; at from 7s. 3d. to 9s. 7d. in France, Belgium, and Germany ; at from 2s. 4d. to 2s. 11d. in Russia, the one thing which was most dreaded by the Continental manufacturers everywhere was British competition. The demand for Protection was loudest in France, Austria, and Russia, where the average wages reached their minimum.'

Mr. Rendel, acting on behalf of many leading Railway Companies in India, placed large contracts for locomotives in England, as being far more cheaply produced in this country than elsewhere, His experience was by no means limited to the purchase of locomotives. Rails and iron-bridge work upon the largest scale had been supplied in England for the Indian railways for which he had acted. Tenders were obtained on all occasions, when a large order had been given, by open advertisement ; and all Continental makers had been as free to tender and would be accepted on the same guarantees as English makers. Yet out of the total expenditure during the ten years preceding the publication of ' Work and Wages ' of from £7,000,000 to £8,000,000 sterling on materials and plant for the East Indian railways constructed under Mr. Rendel's super-vision, with the exceptions I have made, the whole of these contracts had been obtained by English manufacturers.

Another interesting and conclusive proof of the success with which our engine-builders could compete for the supply of locomotives was furnished by the following schedule, prepared by Mr. W. P. Andrew, of the tenders for ninety-four locomotives received by the Punjaub Railway Company in answer to a public advertisement in January 1866 :—

Tenders for Supply of Engines for the Punjaub Railway.

Country from which tender received	Price per engine and tender
1. Germany	£3156
2. England	2990
3. England	2960
4. England	2950
5. England	2850
6. England	2835
7. England	2810
8. England	2790
9. England	2750
10. Germany	2750
11. England	2685
12. Germany	2680
13. England	2680
14. Switzerland	2650
15. England	2650
16. England	2600
17. France	2595
18. England	2575
19. England	2500
20. Scotland	2424
21. Scotland	2395

Serious alarm was felt when, in 1865, fifteen engines were ordered for the Great Eastern Railway from MM. Schneider. These misgivings would probably have been allayed had it been generally known that at the same time when the fifteen engines were ordered from Creuzot forty other engines were ordered from English firms, and that when MM. Schneider were subsequently asked to undertake the construction of twenty-five more engines at the price they had agreed to accept for the fifteen engines originally ordered the offer was declined.

The prices actually quoted by the various tenders are given in the following table :—

Tenders for Fifty-five Goods and Twenty-five Passenger Engines, June 1865.

	Goods	Passenger	Mean
English makers . .	£3350	£3350	£3350
,, ,, . .	3300	3350	3325
,, . .	3250	3200	3225
	3145	3085	3115
	3115	3085	3100
	3045	3135	3090
	3100	3075	3088
,, ,, . .	No tender	2950	—
,, ,, .	2950	2940	2945
Belgian makers . .	2890	2890	2890
English makers . .	2889	2790	2840
,, ,, .	2745	2695	2720
,, ,,	2730	2590	2660
,, ,, . .	2600	No tender	—

Schneider, Tender for Goods and Passenger Engines, together, £2498.

	Goods	Passenger	Delivered in
English makers . .	2395	2280	Liverpool
,, ,, . .	2450	2300	,,
,, . .	2575	2240	,,
,, . .	2600	2400	,,
.. . .	2950	2700	Poti

The extent to which our engine-building establishments were employed upon foreign orders may
be proved by a comparison of their actual capabilities
with the following estimate of the home demand for
locomotives. In the year 1865 Mr. Manby found,
from careful analysis of returns made to him from
numerous railways, that the life of engines built
by Messrs. Robert Stephenson and Co. might be
taken at 480,000 miles. At that period the
'train mileage' of the United Kingdom equalled
120,000,000 miles. Then 120,000,000 ÷ 480,000 =
250 + 50 engines (for contingencies) = 300 engines
worn out annually. Since the date of Mr. Manby's
calculation railway traffic has been enormously
increased.

The eminent English engineer at whose instance
the original order was entrusted to MM. Schneider
possessed, from long residence in France, a special
knowledge of French workmen ; and it was his
opinion that the price of that kind of labour in
France was not generally cheaper for a given quantity
of work than it was in England, while the material
of course cost at least as much.

In an interesting report on Belgian industry Lord
Howard de Walden remarked that the Belgians exhibited their greatest qualities in the manufacture
of arms at Liège. 'In all works in sheet-iron, for
example stoves, the Belgians excel ; but in wrought-
iron they are behind many other countries. A good
lock and key is nowhere to be found. It is cheaper
to buy one of English make. A tolerable horseshoe
is nowhere to be seen, nor are the agricultural

implements of good quality, and yet in carriage-building they have been eminently successful.'

As practical mechanics the English are unsurpassed. The presence of the English engineer, the solitary representative among a crew of foreigners of the mechanical genius of his country, is a familiar recollection to all who have travelled by sea. Consul Lever, in his report of 1870 from Trieste, says that in the vast establishment of the Austrian Lloyds at that port a number of English mechanical engineers are employed not only in the workshops but as navigating engineers in the company's fleet. Although there is no difficulty in substituting for these men Germans and Swiss at lower rates of payment, the uniform accuracy of the English, their intelligence, their consummate mastery of all the details of their art, and their resource in every case of difficulty have entirely established their superiority.

The building and working of steamers involve expenditure in almost all descriptions of labour—the purchase of raw materials of every kind, as well as the most elaborate machinery.

Mining is perhaps the most exhausting and laborious of occupations. The English miner surpasses the foreigner all over the world. On the Continent, long after earthwork and other operations involved in the construction of railways had been committed to the native workmen, English miners were still employed in the tunnels. In making the railway from Chambéry, in Savoy, to the foot of Mont Cenis, Piedmontese were employed in the comparatively easy work of tunnelling in the dry rock ; Englishmen were still required in soft and yielding clay, subject to a constant influx of water.

Mr. Kitson, of Leeds, in his evidence before the Select Committee on Scientific Instruction in 1868, stated that in 1864, in consequence of a dispute with the workmen at Leeds, he had engaged several Frenchmen and Belgians. This experiment proved that the ' foreign workmen were scarcely as intelligent as our own.' ' We are not,' he said, ' inferior in the manufacture of iron, machinery, and steel to the foreign ironmasters. The English are equal to the Belgians in the manufacture of iron, and are superior in the manufacture of machinery.'

At locomotive-building works in Belgium the work was rarely executed with the same precision as in England. All the parts of English engines made from the same pattern are interchangeable. This was not always the case in Belgian engines.

It had been objected that Belgian rails were being largely imported into England. It is true that some 600 tons for the East Gloucestershire Railway were supplied by a Belgian firm in 1865. The price of these rails was £6 10s. per ton, delivered at Gloucester. A solitary instance proves nothing as to general comparative prices. It was because our ironmasters were more fully employed than the ironmasters in Belgium, and because the prices of rails had in consequence fallen more rapidly in Belgium than in England, that the order in question was executed abroad. Since the year 1865 rails have been made in England at a cheaper rate than that paid for the Belgian rails supplied to the East Gloucestershire Railway.

The fortunes of our Belgian rivals have been as chequered as those of their English ironmasters. The following table shows the fluctuations in Belgian prices :—

Average Price per Ton of Belgian Rails.

				Francs
For 1835, average price per ton	.	.	.	340,00
,, 1836 ,, ,,	.	.	.	425,00
, 1837 ,,	.	.	.	438,75
, 1838 ,,	.	.	.	394,00
, 1839 ,,	.	.	.	378,00
, 1840 ,,	.	.	.	239,50
, 1841 ,,	.	.	.	248,00
, 1842 ,,	.	.	.	234,00
, 1843 ,,	.	.	.	221,60
, 1844 ,,	.	.	.	290,00
, 1845 ,,	.	.	.	309,00
, 1846 ,,	.	.	.	320,00
, 1847 ,,	.	.	.	263,00
, 1848 ,,	.	.	.	190,00
, 1849 ,,	.	.	.	180,00
, 1850 ,,	.	.	.	170,00
, 1851 ,,	.	.	.	170,00
, 1852 ,,	.	.	.	172,00
, 1853 ,,	.	.	.	231,00
, 1854 ,,	.	.	.	220,25
, 1855 ,,	.	.	.	212,50
, 1856 ,,	.	.	.	213,85
, 1857 ,,	.	.	.	237,65
, 1858 ,,	.	.	.	160,00
, 1859 ,,	.	.	.	160,00
,, 1860 ,,	.	.	.	160,30
, 1861 ,,	.	.	.	156,85

Average Price per Ton of Belgian Rails.

			Francs
For 1862, average price per ton . . .	149,60
„ 1863 „ „ . . .	142,90
, 1864 „ . . .	157,35
, 1865 „ . . .	162,65
, 1866 „ . . .	169,00
„ 1867 „ . . .	137,70
„ 1868 „ „ . . .	170,80

Much has been said, too, from time to time as to the importation of iron girders from Belgium into this country. Dr. Percy, in his evidence before the Committee on Scientific Education, stated that the iron girders imported from Belgium would be made here if there were a larger demand. A manufacturer would not alter his mills for a special kind of girder unless there was considerable demand. He urged, as a sufficient reason why there should be no apprehension on this subject, the remarkable success which had been achieved in England in the production of armour-plates. It was well known that in 1869 the productive powers of our rail-rolling mills were strained to the utmost, and that almost the whole of those rails were exported.

CHAPTER IV

CO-OPERATIVE PRODUCTION

Address to the Annual Conference of the Co-operative Societies at Halifax, April 6, 1874.

THE main purpose of the friends of the co-operative movement is to secure to the great body of consumers the means of obtaining the necessaries of life at the lowest practicable cost, and of the best quality. So long as this object is attained, it matters not whether it be accomplished through the co-operative associations, or by the agency of the ordinary retailer.

The problem of co-operative production still awaits solution. The equitable distribution of profits between labour, capital, and the inventive faculty, which creates, and the commercial and organising faculty, which conducts, a business, is the most important, as it is undoubtedly one of the most difficult, of the social problems of our age.

Many think that in the actual organisation of productive industry there is a disproportionate assignment of profits to capital. As instances of individual success are multiplied, so this conviction of the injustice of the existing order of things in the commercial world will be strengthened and confirmed. We may be able to prove that the capital of the large capitalist ordinarily receives but a

Inequalit of wealth

E

moderate return, and indeed is freely employed on easier terms than a needy man would exact ; but it is not less true that, measured by the strict necessities of life, an accumulation of wealth must, under all circumstances, be a superfluity. The sentiments so naturally aroused by the spectacle of this ungracious contrast between wealth and poverty have found an illustrious, though not unprejudiced, exponent in the poet Wordsworth :

Slaves cannot breathe in England—yet that boast
Is but a mockery ! when from coast to coast,
Though fettered slaves be none, her floors and soil
Groan underneath a weight of slavish toil,
For the poor many, measured out by rules
Fetched with cupidity from heartless schools,
That to an idol, falsely called ‘ The Wealth
Of Nations,’ sacrifice a people’s health,
Body and mind and soul ; a thirst so keen
Is ever urging on the vast machine
Of sleepless Labour, ’mid whose dizzy wheels
The power least prized is that which thinks and feels.

Socialism is the protest of labour against the unequal distribution of the profits of production. There cannot be equality in a society composed of individuals unequally endowed in knowledge, natural aptitude, and in physical and mental power. But while there cannot be equality, there must be justice.

Co-opera-
tive pro-
duction.
Viewing the subject in the light indicated in these observations, success is much to be desired for the experiment of adapting the co-operative principle to productive industry. In a co-operative mill, or workshop, or farm, the producers unite the double

functions of capital and labour. The handicraftsman sits in judgment on the claims of the capital
provided by his own thrift and past labours. He
is not likely to appropriate an inadequate rate of
interest to a fund obtained from such a source.
He cannot, at the same time, apportion too much
to capital without doing an injustice to himself in
another capacity.

In the co-operative establishments there cannot,
in the nature of things, be contention between a
body of workmen and an individual whom they
regard with unfriendly eyes as a selfish monopolist.
Nor will the benefits be confined to co-operative
establishments alone. Disputes relating to wages
will be more easily adjusted when the capitalist is
enabled to refer the labourer to the rates of wages
prevailing in co-operative establishments, where
they have been determined, not by a single individual suspected of being without sympathy for
the labourer, but by men who, in the capacity of
workmen, become the earners of wages fixed and
paid by themselves.

The desideratum in all labour disputes is a
standard set up by an impartial tribunal, by which
it may readily be decided what constitutes a fair
rate of wages. When co-operative production has
been introduced into all branches of industry
successfully and on a sufficiently extensive scale,
we shall have the universal gauge or measure of the
workman's rightful claims. From the day when
the workman will take his part in the deliberations
which accord to capital its fair rate of interest, and

A stan-
dard of
wages re-
quired.

to the wage-earner his due ; from the day when the workman may count with certainty on a just and equal participation in the profits of every enterprise in which he is engaged in proportion to his merits, we may venture to hope that strikes will cease and that workmen will be content to devote themselves to the successful prosecution of the industry in which they find their employment. If it should appear an exaggeration of the powers of human nature to adopt the principles on which Fourier insisted and to regard all labour as a pleasure, it is possible to conceive conditions in which labour would appear more attractive than hitherto. The labourer might have more satisfaction in working under the direction of persons selected by himself than he now experiences under the authority of an employer upon whom he is entirely dependent as the distributor of wages.

Advocates of the labour interest insist that among capitalists there is a universal desire to acquire wealth, and but little disposition to pay due regard to the rights of others. There may be cases in which these allegations are true. They do not correctly represent the general tone and temper of the employers of this country. In France and Germany similar representations have gained many credulous converts. In those countries, and especially in the former, there is much hostility between masters and men. Even when kind and considerate acts are done they are regarded with suspicion. There is no such hostility of class and class in this country. That it does not exist is conclusively proved by the support given by multitudes of working men at the recent general election to Conservative candidates, who, among other claims to favour, are supposed to be the chosen defenders of the rights of property.

The disposition to be liberal towards workmen is developed, as a general rule, in proportion to the extent of the business and the capital of the employer. The love of gain is strongest among certain smaller employers. The least generous members of the class are often those who have most recently raised themselves from the capacity of workmen to that of employers.

There is a power for good in large accumulations of capital in the hands of a single individual resolved to make a right use of his resources. It is by such men that some of the most judicious operations have been carried out in this country for developing the mineral resources of an untried district, for the advancement of agriculture by costly drainage, for the comfort of the poor by the erection of convenient dwelling-houses, for the improvement of our towns and cities by the destruction of unwholesome habitations and the erection of dwellings furnished with all the contrivances of modern sanitary science, and for the extension of the boon of railway communication into thinly peopled districts. Works such as these, however profitable in the long run, generally involve a protracted lock-up of capital, which the ordinary investor, who cannot afford to lose for a long period the interest upon a comparatively slender capital, is unable to bear.

Apart, however, from such exceptional cases, the
argument in favour of a more equal participation in
profits is incontrovertible.　The co-operative system
of production leads us that way.　In its practical
application there are grave difficulties.　In delibera-
tion the opinions of many counsellors serve to
establish sound conclusions in the mind.　To govern
and administer, all experience proves the infinite
superiority of individual over corporate management.　'There be three points of business,' says
Lord Bacon—'the preparation, the debate or
examination, and the perfection.　Whereof, if you
look for despatch, let the middle only be the work
of many, and the first and last the work of few.'

The following opinion of Mr. Erastus Bigelow, of
Massachusetts, quoted by Mr. Harris Gastrell, may
appropriately be cited :—' The Corporation system
has been a serious hindrance to the proper diversifi-
cation of our manufactures. . . . I will point out
briefly some of the disadvantages.　When men who
are occupied with other pursuits decide to invest
capital in manufacturing corporations it is usually
done on grounds of general confidence.　They invest
because others are investing.　They believe, without
exactly knowing why, that such investments are
safe, and will be profitable ; or they follow the lead
of some friend, in whose knowledge and judgment
they confide.　They do not act on their own acquaintance with the nature and requirements of the
business ; for such an acquaintance can be made
only by careful investigation or actual experience.
The natural consequence of all this is that capital

for the extension of old or the projection of new manufacturing enterprises can seldom be obtained at those times when it is most needed and might most profitably be employed. This single feature of the system is fatal to any true and healthy progress under it.

' The capital thus raised must be expended. An agent is employed and enters on his work. Those capitalists who have invested under the stimulus of high profits are impatient for results, and urge him to hasty action on ill-considered plans. A sudden and unnatural demand for operatives is thus created, raising the rate of wages and greatly enhancing the cost of goods. Lastly, unity of purpose and action, without which no business can be successfully prosecuted, can hardly be expected under the divided responsibilities of a large corporate organisation.'

A ready means of applying the principle of limited liability to all descriptions of business was created by the Joint Stock Companies Act of 1862. That enactment gave great facilities for the sale of their property to joint-stock companies to men at the head of large concerns, who were tired of hard work, and anxious to hand down to their families an inheritance secured from the risks and fluctuations of trade.

Losses in joint-stock companies.

While there were many seeking to exchange the wear and tear of business for the comparatively easy life of the country gentleman, there was a large body of inexperienced and sanguine investors who had deluded themselves with the belief that it was possible to conduct the most intricate operations

of industry successfully without experience **and**
without that constant personal devotion to administrative details which the individual manufacturers whose property they had purchased had
found it essential to bestow.   In numerous instances
the purchasers have sustained a serious loss.   The
explanation is not rarely to be found in the im-
perfect control exercised by a board of directors,
assisted by a salaried manager, as compared with
the administration of the individual employers.

Business of a rail-way con-tractor could not be man-aged by a company.

Even in the choice of an agent, representative, or
manager, a private individual has advantages over a
board.   Take the case of a railway contractor.   The
contracts for a long line of railway are subdivided,
for the purposes of the supervision of the work,
into sections rarely exceeding eight to ten miles
in length.   If the works are unusually heavy the
sections are shorter in proportion.   A sub-agent
is placed in charge of each section, and an experienced agent has the general direction of the whole
contract.   The principal contractor for the undertaking, by paying frequent visits of inspection, has
opportunities of becoming acquainted with every
sub-agent in his employ.   He observes the progress
made on his section.   He can test his capability of
dealing with every kind of practical engineering
difficulty by moving him from railway to railway,
and putting him in charge of work in districts totally
dissimilar in their physical character and resources.
Gradually those employed in a subordinate capacity
have an opportunity of showing their powers.
There is ample scope for individual merit.   The

supervision of the agent having the general charge will prevent the mistakes of a subordinate from producing very serious consequences. Thus, with the lapse of time, and without any grave risk of loss, the contractor may form an opinion as to who are his most trustworthy sub-agents, and can select principal agents from among their number with confidence, their powers having been thoroughly tested in a subordinate capacity. Here it will be obvious that long experience and continuity of management are essential. A board will make appointments upon the faith of testimonials. The private individual will trust to personal observation.

Again, administrative success depends upon the knowledge and management of details. The art of organising large bodies of workmen will only be obtained by previous experience on a smaller scale. The general supervision of subordinates will be most effectually exercised by one who, by close observation on the spot, whether in the tunnel, the workshop, or the factory, has learned how to discharge in his own person the duty he has delegated to others. The greatest commanders and administrators have ever been consummate masters of detail. Napoleon's arrangements for the marches undertaken by his vast armies are admirable for the forethought and the care wisely bestowed upon details. A council or a board, only occasionally meeting, cannot manage a business. Unless efficiently represented by their officers and servants, they are practically powerless. In a commercial point of view, great profits in productive industry are generally obtained by infinite small economies. Directors in a board-room can effect nothing in this way. Every economy of expenditure must be suggested by close and constant observation of the processes by which materials are prepared, and labour applied to the execution of the work.

Managers must be liberally paid. In the organisation of co-operative production it is essential to secure the services of individuals competent to take the general management. The manual operations will be skilfully and probably more diligently performed in a co-operative esta-blishment. The personal interests of the work-men will be so directly advanced by their application and perseverance, that they will naturally work hard. Their best efforts will fail to ensure a satis-factory result, unless the general organisation is perfect also.

This organising faculty is a rare gift. It must be combined with long experience and excellent judg-ment, or the commercial result cannot be satis-factory. Many possess, in an eminent degree, inventive skill. Others have powers of persuasive speech, which enable them for a time to command great influence in financial circles. When, however, they come to deal with practical questions, they fail. Mechanical and scientific ability will not command success unless united with prudence and tact. High diplomatic qualities are often required in the conduct of negotiations, both with the trade out of doors and with the workmen employed. Above all, there must be integrity and high-minded resolution to withstand the temptations that come from the love of money and operate so strongly on the minds of men of slender means and great ambition.

We have the most conclusive evidence that the administrative powers, of which I speak, are as rare as they are essential, in the handsome salaries which men possessing such qualifications often obtain, not only as managers of large joint-stock companies, but in the employ of private firms. When shall we find co-operative shareholders ready to give £5000 a year for a competent manager ? And yet the sum I have named is readily paid by private employers to an able lieutenant.

It is because there has been in co-operative establishments a reluctance to pay what is necessary to enlist first-rate ability in the management of the business, that their operations have hitherto been attended with very partial success. Only personal experience of the difficulties of the task would induce a body of workmen to reserve from their earnings a sum sufficient to secure the services of competent leaders.

Those interested in co-operative production should not commence on a large scale a business difficult to manage. A moderate capital is easily obtained. Large funds are not rapidly procured. Where only a few hands are engaged, the government may be conducted on a purely democratic basis. Where the energies of a multitude are to be combined, there must be an enlightened despotism.

In the case of a co-operative establishment, the

Co-operative production should be on a small scale.

persons entrusted with plenary powers must, as a
matter of course, be subject to the control of the
contributors of the capital. Their control should
be exercised only at stated, though sufficiently
frequent, intervals. It was rightly pointed out
by Mr. Morrison, in the debates at the last Conference of Co-operative Societies, that, without
the concentration of management among a limited
number of persons, it would be impossible to preserve
the unity of tradition and administration, so essential to establish the reputation of a factory or
workshop, and to secure the high prices consumers
are always ready to pay for goods of undoubted
quality.

The appointment of the manager by popular
election—the electors being the hand workers, who
are to serve under the chief, selected by themselves—
is not incompatible with continuity of management.
In a trading concern the acting partner or manager,
who has personal control, is rarely obtained by
hereditary succession. It is seldom that a man of
commercial genius has a worthy successor in his son.
The elective principle will be at least as well calculated as the hereditary to protect the workmen
from the disasters which must inevitably be caused
by incapacity in the management.

Co-operative societies of production would
doubtless have been established far more rapidly,
unless there had been formidable difficulties to be
surmounted. The most recent report shows that
the number of these societies may almost be counted
on the fingers. Though some of the experiments

actually tried have been successful, the failures have been more numerous than the successes. The Paisley Manufacturing Society, the Hebden Bridge Fustian Society, the Eccles Quilt Manufacturing Society, the Lurgan Damask Manufacturing Society, are examples of co-operative production successfully conducted, but on a small scale. The promoters have wisely held back from attempting more ambitious undertakings. The Printing Society of Manchester is a greater effort, and it is highly flourishing. It is possible that the business is of a kind which depends less on the administrative ability of the manager than on the individual exertions of the workmen. The Co-operative Printing Society recently established in London has failed to command a remunerative business.

The most important experiment in co-operative Ouseburn production hitherto attempted in this country is that of the Ouseburn Engine Works. This Company has sustained a severe loss ; strikes for higher wages on the part of the workmen employed in one department of the concern. The occurrence of a strike in a co-operative establishment proves the difficulty, though not the impossibility, of conducting an undertaking on a democratic system, when you have to deal with many classes of workmen, possessing different and unequal qualifications.

The adjustment of the rates of wages in a case in which some members of the co-operative body must be paid at considerably higher rates than others, requires on the part of the latter no common measure of self-denial. It is sometimes hard to recognise the superior merits of others, even when we have the means of forming an independent opinion on their claims ; but when workmen, brought up in one trade, are required to assign much higher wages to artisans practising another trade, of the exact nature and difficulty of which they have no experience, they are naturally slow to recognise what is due to superior skill.

In the case of the Ouseburn Company, the causes of the early losses were explained by Dr. Rutherford in his speech delivered on the occasion of the visit of this Congress to the works, at their last conference. Orders had been booked at too low a price. The manager, by whom the directors were advised, was much at fault. The head of the undertaking should have been, as Dr. Rutherford so justly urged, a practical engineer, as well as a philanthropist. To secure the services of a competent manager the remuneration required should have been measured, not by a few hundred, but by a few thousand pounds. The history of the Ouseburn works is an illustration of the principles already laid down. The early failure is attributable to the want of that experience and technical and practical knowledge, which can only be supplied by the appointment of a highly qualified engineer. When such a man has been found, all will go well with the Ouseburn Company.

The valuable reports of Her Majesty's Secretaries of Legation describe many successful applications of the co-operative principle which may prove encouraging to English enterprise.

It is stated by Mr. Ford that the Executive Committee of the Tailors' Union in New York, on notifying the cessation of a strike, in which the trade had been engaged in 1869, declared that their policy would thenceforward be to abandon the system of strikes, and to fight with the stronger weapon of co-operation. Co-operation in United States.

The co-operative principle has been adopted by those strange religious sects, the Mormons, Shakers, Economists, and Perfectionists. They have attained to great success in the organisation of labour. The Mormons at Salt Lake City have transformed ' a wilderness into a garden,' and I can speak from personal knowledge when I say that the Shakers are excellent farmers.

Co-operative foundries have been established in New York and Massachusetts. There is an Iron Foundry at Troy, in New York, which was started in May 1866, with a capital of £2700 paid up. The shares were fixed at £20, and limited in number to 2000. In the first year thirty-two men, in the second seventy-five, in 1869 eighty-five men were employed in the works. A dividend of 10 per cent. was made in the first year, and 30 per cent. more was paid on labour. The second year the dividends on stock and labour amounted to 89 per cent. In 1869 they reached 100 per cent. The most skilled trades earn, owing to their steady employment, 35 per cent. more than the same classes of workmen would earn at similar wages in any private foundry. Great economy has been effected in the use of materials, and the strictest discipline is enforced.

Up to the date of Mr. Ford's report, all the profits due to individuals had been paid to them in shares, with the view of applying the additional capital to the enlargement of the works.

The co-operative movement, thus happily begun, has been followed up with energy and spirit. Mr. Archibald, our Consul-General in New York, writing in 1872, says : ' During the past year, co-operative concerns have been organised in several departments of business, but with far greater success in industrial than in commercial matters. The Working Men's Manufacturing Company, with a capital of £25,000, has been formed at Emmaus. It is to be conducted on the co-operative principle, and will erect extensive works, including a foundry, forge, and two machine shops, employing at the commencement about 200 hands.'

Vienna. In Austria, the majority of the printers, though in theory advocates of the views of Lassalle in favour of Government workshops, in practice have adopted the sound doctrine inculcated by Schulze-Delitzsch, the eminent German economist, that every man should trust to self-help, rather than place his dependence on the Government. The printers of Vienna have established a co-operative press. Lord Lytton states in his report that 1500 printers were, in 1869, negotiating for the purchase of another office.

Sweden. Mr. Jocelyn, in his report of 1869, refers to the progress of co-operative production in Sweden. This most difficult form of labour organisation has been particularly successful in that country. He attributes this fortunate result to a spirit of independence highly honourable to the Swedish workmen. They will willingly risk their savings for the sake of seizing an opportunity of rising from a dependent position to the freedom of co-operative industry. It has been found in Sweden that the smaller undertakings of this nature are the most prosperous. Where, on the other hand, many are associated upon an equal footing for the promotion of manufactures requiring unusual skill, there is great danger of the whole becoming *de facto* the property of a few of the original founders, while the rest sink back into the condition of simple workmen under their command.

While the efforts to establish co-operative production in this country have not thus far been attended with a large measure of success, the importance of the principle is so great, let us deprecate the abandonment of further attempts in the same direction. The wiser course will be to avoid, as it has been already suggested, commencing undertakings on a large scale.

When the business is of a kind that cannot be carried out advantageously on a moderate footing, the co-operative principle should be applied to the execution of sub-contracts for portions of the work, to the supply of a part of a large order, or to the execution of a single process in a complicated manufacture. Let us take the business of a railway contractor. When a railway contract has been entered into, the principal contractor usually subdivides the works, and lets them out to sub-con-

F

tractors.   On a long line of railway cutting, bridges,
tunnels, embankments, and stations are executed
by one or more separate contractors ; and thus the
co-operative system may readily be applied to the
construction of every section of the largest undertaking, after it has been sufficiently subdivided.
The same remarks apply to shipbuilding and many
other branches of industry, where the subdivision
of the work will give ample scope for the application
of the co-operative system, combined and organised
under an employer of superior administrative skill
and large resources.

Sub-con-
tracts.

It may be interesting to men who are engaged in
a great effort to organise a new and better system
for the application of capital and labour to production, to hear some details of the methods adopted
by the English contractors who have been engaged
in the execution of great railway contracts both at
home and abroad.   In the conduct of these works
the main object in view has been to give to the
workmen a personal interest in the performance of
an adequate quantity of work, in return for the wages
received.   In the case of the contractor, it was
especially important to attain this object by making
it the interest of the labourer to do his fair share
of work, rather than by placing reliance on a
close personal inspection of his conduct.   With the
development of railway enterprise, the practice was
adopted of inviting English contractors with competent resources to undertake railway and other
works, not only in their own country, but in every
quarter of the globe.   The difficulties of super-

vision of necessity increased with the enlarged area
of their operations.   It was essential to devise some
plan by which it should, if possible, be made an
advantage to every individual concerned to perform
his share of the common task to the best of his
ability.

Thus the system of sub-contract and piece-work,
originally adopted by the pioneers of railway construction, was extended to every operation where
it was possible to apply it.   The general character
of the arrangements may perhaps be best explained
by the selection of an example taken from actual
practice.   On the contract for part of the London
and South Western Railway between Basingstoke
and Winchester there was an unusual proportion
of excavation, amounting to some $3\frac{1}{4}$ millions of cubic
yards on a length of eighteen miles.   Not only were
the works of a heavy and costly nature, but the
time allowed for the completion was so short as to
render the utmost diligence and energy necessary.
The operations were carried on night and day, and
1100 workmen were employed.

There was one cutting of unusual dimensions near
Winchester, which, in the deepest part, was from
90 to 100 feet in depth.   Here, in spite of severe and
unfavourable weather, the works were pushed on
with the utmost diligence and determination.   This
was done even at a considerable pecuniary sacrifice.
The contractor was anxious, above all things, to
maintain and increase the good reputation he had
already begun to establish, and of which he was
wisely jealous as the surest guarantee for his future

success.   At Micheldever there was one immense embankment, about 85 feet in height ; and at Popham Beacons a short cutting, not more than 10 chains in length, intervening between two tunnels, of such a depth that 100,000 cubic yards were excavated in order to make the cutting.

The whole of these works were executed by sub-contract.   The amount of work let to a particular sub-contractor was determined by the appreciation formed by the principal contractor or his agent of the ability of the individual to carry out the work. A man of superior qualifications was allowed to take a sub-contract for an amount of work increasing in magnitude in proportion to the confidence entertained in his ability.   Some of the sub-contractors would take contracts for work costing in the total £15,000 to £20,000, and employing from 150 to 200 men.

Frequently the sub-contractor would again let his work to the navvies at so much a yard.   They worked in what were called butty gangs, or parties of from six to twelve men.   The navvies would take a contract under a sub-contractor for excavating so many yards of earth at so much per yard, dividing the earnings equally amongst each other. Disputes would frequently arise between the butty gangs and the sub-contractors upon the question of measurement.   In such cases the resident agent or representative of the principal contractor was required to arbitrate.

When the work was organised in the manner I have described, the function of the principal contractor was rather that of practical engineer superintending the execution of the works by a number of smaller contractors. The principal contractor, being responsible to the engineer for the faithful performance of the contract, would watch the work done by the sub-contractors, and see that it was executed in such a manner as to satisfy the requirements of the engineer. He was not directly the employer of the workmen or the navvies. The policy was to avoid, as far as possible, engaging a large number of workmen by the day, and to pay every man concerned in proportion to results.

> If little labour, little are our gains,
> Man's fortunes are according to his pains.

The system of sub-contract was carried so far that I have been informed by Mr. Harrison, the experienced contractor from whom I have derived the facts already quoted, that the very scaffolding raised for the purpose of putting together the iron-work of the bridges of the Severn Valley Railway was mostly erected by sub-contractors. A carpenter would take a sub-contract for the erection of such scaffolding, fixing his price by the cubic foot.

Sub-contracts are much approved in the best shipbuilding yards. The following observations, coming from one of the most eminent shipbuilders in the United Kingdom, will be perused with interest by students of the labour problem, whether from a speculative or a practical point of view.

Piece-work in ship-building.

The opinions of the writer from whom I quote fully substantiate the conclusions drawn by my father from a large experience in a totally different field of industry :

'The book and pamphlet on "Work and Wages" you kindly gave me have interested me very much, and directed my attention *particularly* to the past and present of my trades. I say "particularly" as, although I knew roughly how they stood, your writings set me to make out with considerable, if not perfect, accuracy some statistics which I felt sure would interest you as much as myself. I have, accordingly, put these into shape, premising you are at liberty to use them in your "work," but without mentioning names or otherwise, further than as illustrating your views. The businesses in which I am directly or indirectly engaged are shipbuilding, engineering, forging and founding— in fact, everything to complete steamships from the rough cast of malleable iron. I have seen no reason to regret keeping these several departments under separate heads and management.

'I purpose, however, now taking up iron ship-building only, as being much the largest department, and to compare two distinct periods or years— 1868 and 1873. In 1868 we had no piece-work. Between then and 1873 we introduced it, with some little difficulty, into the iron department and black-smith work. We have not yet succeeded in bringing it into play in the ship-carpenter and joiner and some minor branches, but we bide our time. Fully half our pays go to piece-work, leaving the balance for time payment. It is because we only build high-class passenger steamships that we continue to pay

so large a number of men by the day rather than
by the piece. I may observe that the wood department runs much higher in proportion to iron than
in yards mostly devoted to sailing ships or cargo
steamers. The steamships we built in 1868 and
1873 were almost identical in style of finish though
differing in tonnage. We had much trouble about
1868 with our iron hands. It was difficult to get
men, the demand exceeding the supply. The
introduction of the piece system—that is to say,
the payment by results—led to hard, or at least
fairly hard, work on the part of the skilled men,
and to ingenuity on their part and ours to save
unskilled labour by the introduction of machinery.
The result has been that skilled and unskilled men
make 50 per cent. to 75 per cent. more earnings.
We get the work per ton of iron in the ships about
20 per cent. cheaper ; and, from a much smaller
number of men being required, the supply is approximately equal to the demand. Since we introduced piece-work we can estimate to within a
fraction what the iron and blacksmith work will
cost, and we could never do so before. Here I would
observe that all this has been accomplished with
working time in 1873 reduced to 54 hours per week,
whereas in 1868 the men worked 60 hours a week.
As to the skilled hands—and they are all highly
skilled men—in the wood departments, we had to
pay higher wages in 1873 for 54 hours' work than
in 1868 with 60 hours'. We have, however, met
this by the introduction of machinery. Our joinery
and cabinet department is now like an engineer's

shop, with tools for *every description of work.*
I may say in every part of our work, during the
past three or four years, we have been introducing
" steam " and other appliances where we could ;
and there has been generally sharper supervision
and attention on the part of those in charge, and
our manager over them.

'I may now come to results. In 1868 we
launched nine steamships, in round numbers aggregating 13,000 tons. I take gross new measurement in each case for the purpose of comparison.
The wages bill was £78,963 ; average number of
men and boys employed, 1776. In 1873 we
launched seven steamships, in round numbers
aggregating 18,500 tons ; wages bill, £91,838 ;
average number of men and boys employed, 1550.
In 1868 the average wage earned per week of 60
hours was about 17*s*. 1*d*. In 1873, per week of
54 hours, about 22*s*. 9*d*. In 1873 the cost per ton,
gross new measurement, in wages only, was fully
20*s*. cheaper than in 1868, but this reduction is
due to the piece-work departments. We consider it
something to have met the increase in wages and
diminution in hours of the " time-workers " by the
means already mentioned.

'I am not clear that these time-workers work
harder whilst they are at it than they did before
the advance in wages and the decrease in hours, but
we may have gained something from sharper over-
looking. As I have said, we have effected considerable economies by the introduction of steam
machinery and other labour-saving appliances.

'The piece-work system keeps us clearer of disputes and trouble with our men than we were under the old method ; and men and employers alike make a better result. I look to " payment by results " as a system calculated to put an end to many trade disturbances, but trades unions are opposed to it. As ours is practically a non-union yard, we hope in time to overcome the obstacles in our way, and to make the one system universal. Piece-work in the iron department of shipbuilding is now general in the Clyde district.

'As this year will complete my thirtieth in the employment of labour, you will see that my experience of it is somewhat large.'

With these encouraging examples before them, many employers may be glad to follow the same course. No plan by which workmen may be made to realise that they row in the same boat with their employers should be lightly set aside. It is good policy to give up a portion of the profits of a prosperous year in order to avert the calamity of a strike, with all its attendant evils of loss of profit and bitterness and strife between masters and men. Capital and labour are essentially necessary and interdependent elements of production ; and the man of business, not less than the philanthropist, must desire to see the representatives of the two interests closely allied. It has seemed well to remind this Conference of these and other efforts to combine the principle of co-operation with the undoubted advantages of undivided responsibility in the administration of a large undertaking. The corporate system is not always applicable. Where no special personal influence is needed for the purpose of securing clients and customers, and where the internal economy of an establishment can be conducted by a regular routine, there will be no practical disadvantage in the management of a board or council. But when no transaction can be completed without long and difficult negotiations; when an undertaking is of a kind that cannot be conducted in accordance with fixed rules, and the emergencies, which must from the nature of the case arise, are always unforeseen, and must be met on the spot by an administrator upon whose skill and conduct all will depend—in such a case the co-operative system, pure and simple, becomes impossible; and the ingenuity of masters and workmen, wishing to work together in friendly alliance, should rather be employed to devise schemes, whereby the equitable distribution of profits among the workmen may be combined with the necessary concentration of authority in their employer.

There must always be peculiar advantages in the personal supervision (to borrow a French expression) of an experienced 'chief of industry.' The earlier railways of this country were completed with great expedition. There was an anxious demand for improved arterial communications by the new method, the superiority of which was universally acknowledged, so soon as it had been proved practicable. In those days the difficulties of the pioneers of the railway system were great. The best methods of surmounting the engineering problems encountered were not yet perfectly asoertained. In driving a tunnel through a quicksand, in forming a high embankment, or excavating a deep cutting in treacherous and yielding soil, in carrying a line of railway over the trembling bog, the contractor sometimes endured the mortification of seeing the labour of weeks destroyed in a moment.

When in trouble and anxiety, when a difficulty in the execution of the works presented itself, his representatives on the spot would seek for the valuable advice of their chief. In such an emergency he assumed the management of the works. Nor did they ever recur to him without obtaining valuable counsel, the fruits of a wider and more varied experience than their own. It would, in fact, have been impossible for any individual to accumulate the same knowledge, without having the same exceptional opportunity of keeping a continual watch over a large number of operations simultaneously in progress.

In a time of discouragement the personal visits of the master, the words of kindness to the disheartened workmen, the novel yet practical suggestions evolved from a fresh and vigorous mind, brought to bear upon a problem which had baffled the men more immediately concerned, would never fail to cheer up the industrial army, and arouse them to new and, in the end, always victorious efforts.

These details will have sufficiently explained the relations in which the railway contractor, or any other large employer, should stand to the members of his numerous staff. It seems beyond dispute that no board or council could ever take the place of an individual fitted by character and experience for his work, when such operations as I have described are to be carried out successfully. The inspiration given to subordinates under trying circumstances,

Cases in which co-operative system not practicable.

the stores of knowledge and experience of the engineering art, the confidence imparted to engineers and directors and shareholders by the personal reputation of their contractor—these were advantages inseparable from purely personal management and responsibility, and they never would have been obtained from the cumbrous machinery of a board. For these reasons co-operative organisation will rarely prove effectual. A council of war never fights ; and no difficult task in the field of peaceful labour can be brought to completion without a trusted leader.

M. Renan, in his interesting essay, ' La Réforme intellectuelle et morale,' confirms these observations from the results of French experience :—' Rappelez-vous ce qui a tué toutes les sociétés co-opéra-tives d'ouvriers : l'incapacité de constituer dans de telles sociétés une direction sérieuse, la jalousie contre ceux que la société avait revêtus d'un mandat quelconque, la prétention de les subordonner à leurs mandants, le refus obstiné de leur faire une position digne.'

One more suggestion, and I close my remarks on this aspect of the case. In many descriptions of enterprise the commercial result cannot be ascertained until after an interval of time has elapsed too long to be tolerable to a body of workmen dependent on their weekly wages. I again choose an illustration from the experiences of the railway contractor. Take the case of a concession for a long line of railway on the Continent. The first conception of the project will probably come from some local engineer. He makes a rude preliminary survey of the country to be traversed. He comes to England with his rough studies to seek the financial aid and larger professional experience of one of our eminent engineers or contractors. The negotiations proceed, and the English promoters make a second and a more careful examination of the scheme, involving a repetition of the original survey. Plans and an estimate are prepared at considerable expense, and negotiations are thereupon commenced with the Government within whose territories the proposed railway will pass. Weary months, and sometimes years, elapse before a decision is obtained. Let us assume the decision to have been favourable, and that a concession has been granted. Then follows the execution of the works, which, if the length of the railway is considerable, may probably occupy a period of three years. While the construction is progressing, financial arrangements must be made in order to form a company, to take over the concession from the contractors, and to raise the capital for the line by public subscription. The subscription may possibly be only partly successful. In that event, the contractor must meet a large proportion of the expenditure from his private resources. Before

he has succeeded in disposing of his proportion of
the shares or bonds allotted to him, a European
war may have broken out. In that case, an in-
definite period must elapse before the securities are
realised. This is no imaginary picture. In the
business with which my name is identified, the
history of many transactions is a repetition of the
story I have narrated. It is not an exaggeration
to say that an interval of ten years ordinarily
elapsed between the opening of communications
with the original promoters and the final payment
for the construction of the works. Looking to the
hazards and uncertainties of enterprises of this
·nature, no true friend of the working classes would
recommend them to risk their hard earnings in such
adventures.

The general business of the country, however,
is of a more stable and methodical character, and
better adapted for the application of the co-operative
principle.

There are other developments of the co-operative
principle on which the author insisted in his address,
but on which it is impossible to dwell in this reprint
—economy by buying at the stores, economy in
fuel and cooking, economy of living in flats, united
efforts in forming shops, people's banks, charity
organisation. The independent inquiries recorded
in these pages relate mainly to the reward and the
management of labour.

Abroad, arrangements of · the kind indicated
have been long established in every large town,
and especially in France and Italy, and they have

been found to work most conveniently and economically.

The English have been reproached, perhaps not unjustly, as a nation destitute of resources for amusement. Time given to innocent pleasure is not wasted. There are other things besides fame and money, for which it is worth our while to live. To use the happy phrase of Mr. Goschen, ' a livelihood is not a life.' It is not well to concentrate all the thoughts on work, and take no pains to provide pure and elevating enjoyment.

Let us hope the progress of education in England may not be attended with the regrettable consequences that have followed from a wide diffusion of knowledge in other countries. In the United States, the result of universal education has been to make the native-born Americans averse to manual labour. The dignity of the pen is more highly regarded than that of the hatchet or the hammer. The youths of America universally prefer to take very moderate pay as clerks, rather than earn the wages, double their own in amount, given to skilled artisans. The false estimate they have formed of the prestige of a sedentary occupation is due to their education. Even in Germany it has been found that foremen in workshops, notwithstanding their higher responsibilities, do not receive proportionate wages. The general diffusion of education has made most artisans competent, and has made all desire to undertake duties of supervision, and thus escape manual labour.

Education in Greece being practically gratuitous,

thousands aspire to some calling more intellectual than that of the manual labourer. Hence it is, that while every deputy in the Representative Chambers and every member of the Government is besieged with applications for the smallest posts in the public service, the labour market is largely supplied from Crete and Turkey.

I cannot conclude these observations on the conditions of the labouring classes without reference to the important influence which must follow from the increasing facilities of communication between distant centres of industry. Foreign travel, in former times, was the exclusive privilege of the wealthy. In some later day, when working men begin to circulate more freely from country to country, the class interests which they have in common will inevitably tend to bring them together. They will regard with stronger aversion those national struggles in which, from motives of personal ambition, their rulers in past ages have been too ready to engage. Already we see in Germany a party being formed whose sympathies are for France. The originators of the movement are the artisans in the two countries. As their numbers increase, they may exercise a valuable influence in promoting the blessed work of reconciliation. So, too, between England and the United States, the solidarity of the two peoples is a surer guarantee for a close and permanent alliance than the most elaborate contrivances of diplomacy.

Relations between England and the United States.

Our best authors appeal with equal success to

Anglo-Saxon readers in both hemispheres. In the United States they are welcomed as men of whom the American people are proud. They have conferred distinction on the whole English-speaking race. Our early history, our language, our literature, are links which should unite us together as no other people can be united.

CHAPTER V

FAMILISTÈRE DE GUISE

M. Godin.
Among many recent efforts to ameliorate the condition of the working classes, one of the most original and spirited has been made by Monsieur Godin, the founder of the familistère, or general dwelling-house, for his operatives and their families at Guise. The principles of the scheme, and the mode in which the attempt to develop these principles has been conducted, are set forth by M. Godin in his interesting volume entitled 'Solutions Sociales,' from which the following details are extracted. The originality of the plan and the general idea underlying the whole conception of the founder of the institution, that the condition of the masses can be elevated only by their mutual action for the common good, will be essentially acceptable to the friends of the co-operative movement. Whether the familistère is a judicious application of the principle is another question.

There have been many isolated efforts in France and Belgium to improve the habitations of the working class. At Mülhausen especially a large number of houses for workmen have been erected, constituting what has been called a Cité Ouvrière. M. Godin objects that the dwellings erected at Mülhausen are too cramped in dimensions ; that the workmen having been encouraged to purchase their cottages, the founder of the Cité Ouvrière has lost all power of direction and control ; that the rooms originally barely sufficient for the wants of a family are sublet as lodgings ; that pig-styes are constructed in the tiny garden attached to each cottage ; and that thus dirt and noxious odours are allowed to pervade the suburb. M. Godin, not without some justification, finds fault with the term Cité Ouvrière ; and he, perhaps justly, says that the name implies the separation of those who by their labours are the creators of wealth from those who enjoy the use of that wealth by inheritance or by successful speculation.

A more favourable opinion of the Cité Ouvrière of Mülhausen has been formed by Lord Brabazon, who says, in his able paper on the industrial classes in France, that, ' the condition of the lease granted to the workman allowing him, after a certain number of years, to obtain the freehold of his house, has an immense moral influence. His self-respect increases, and he is enlisted on the side of order. The absence of supervision removes a fruitful source of irritation.' The Cités Ouvrières erected for the workmen of Paris, though possessing every advantage of space, air and light, have never been popular, because the strict discipline maintained— as, for example, the closing of the gates at ten o'clock at night—is an irksome restriction to the excitable and pleasure-seeking population of the French capital.

The criticisms applied to the Cité Ouvrière at

Mülhausen may be applied with greater reason to London and the great towns of our own country. The rich gather together in the most eligible situations. The price of land in certain positions becomes so enormous that it is impossible to erect houses at rates which, while not exceeding what workmen can afford to pay, will be remunerative to the owners and builders. Hence, the working class are compelled to occupy more remote suburbs. They live in daily contact with no other class but their own. A consequent danger is incurred of social disunion. This state of things is practically inevitable under our existing system. It is not the less a regrettable incident of the great increase in our population.

M. Godin suggests that it is a paramount obligation of the wealthy to organise means for securing to the masses a larger measure of the luxury and comfort created by their toil and labour.

The tendency of modern industry has been, and will continue to be, towards the concentration of capital in large private or corporate establishments, and to production by machinery, in substitution for manual labour. The use of machinery necessarily operates unfavourably to the interests of small manufacturers without the resources of capital. This general tendency of our industrial organisation has been promoted by the railway system. Consumers have been enabled to obtain their supplies from the cheapest markets, irrespective of those considerations of transport which in former times more than neutralised the advantages of different localities for special branches of trade. Before the introduction of railways, it was essential to obtain the more bulky articles from the local producer. Now the consumers are enabled to go to the localities where the articles required can be produced of the best quality and at the cheapest rate.

The attention of the employers has hitherto been concentrated on the organisation of the factory and the workshop, on the great scale required in the present day, in order to carry on competition in manufactures with success. Though much has been done to organise the production, nothing has been done to organise the consumption and the use of products.

The problem of domestic consumption has been solved in the opinion of M. Godin by the erection, close to his workshops at Guise, of an edifice which he calls a Social Palace. It is a vast barrack, capable of containing 900 inhabitants. The building is several storeys in height, and consists of three large courts, surrounded by galleries communicating with the rooms. Each room is let separately, so that the lodgers can regulate the rents in exact and constant proportion to their requirements. The unmarried and the married, according to the number of their family, can occupy a greater or lesser number of rooms. The building cost £40,000. The capital expended has been divided into shares of small amount, with the view of inducing the workmen to purchase them, and thus to become their own landlords. The rents of the rooms give a return of 3 per cent. upon the capital. The profit upon the sale of provisions gives an additional percentage of the like amount.

M. Godin quotes the principles advocated by Fourier as the foundation of his system. By grouping many families together, each individual is enabled to undertake, for the general sèrvice of the community, that special function in which he excels. Cooking, and all the domestic duties, may thus be performed by persons specially selected. At the familistère there are general kitchens for the whole establishment, from which the meals ordered by lodgers are supplied. The children, as soon as they can leave their mothers, are brought up first of all in infant schools, and then in more advanced schools, where they receive an excellent education.

It is contended that under this system the working men enjoy by combination many of those advantages which must otherwise be the exclusive privilege of wealth. Cooking is often badly done for the rich ; *a fortiori*, it is to be expected that it will be unskilful in the homes of the poor. To command the services of efficient persons, whether in the capacity of nurses or cooks, is regarded by M. Godin as among the greatest advantages of ample resources. By combination the occupants of the Social Palace at Guise are enabled to place their children, even at a tender age, under the care of well-trained nurses, and to obtain their own food properly cooked.

Where the working men live apart from each other in small houses they are necessarily widely scattered. They are at a distance from their work, and their children are so far from school that their attendance is always difficult and often most irregular.

In case of illness the services of a medical man may not be easily obtained. Nor can medical comforts be provided as in an establishment having a well-equipped dispensary for the general use of the inmates.

The Social Palace at Guise stands in the midst of extensive and well-kept pleasure grounds on the banks of the Oise. It has an excellent theatre, where dramatic representations and concerts are frequently given by associations formed for the purpose by the operatives.

The internal management is carried on by committees composed of twelve men and twelve women. The men devote themselves specially to questions relating to the amelioration of the condition of the workmen, the rates of wages, and the formation of provident societies. The women supervise the quality of the provisions supplied from the co-operative stores and butchers' shops connected with the Social Palace. They also superintend the management of the children and the arrangements for preserving order and cleanliness.

It is alleged that there is an entire absence of crime in this singular community ; and that public opinion, the more sensibly felt when all dwell together under the same roof, has raised the tone of conduct and morals above the standard generally maintained among persons of the same class living in private dwellings.

CHAPTER VI

Trades Union Congress, Leicester, October 1877

BEFORE entering upon more important topics, I desire to express my high appreciation of the honour of being invited to address the Delegates from the Trades Unions at their annual Congress. Connected as I am with the employers of labour, you cannot expect me to come here to encourage an aggressive movement against men of my own order. I shall strive to hold the equal scales of justice as between capital and labour.

I have before had occasion to vindicate the character of the English workman from unmerited strictures. The same charges are renewed to-day, and again I ask for evidence to prove that the English workman is deteriorating. Has the volume of our trade diminished while that of other nations has increased ? This question may be satisfactorily answered by a reference to Mr. Leone Levi's *History of British Commerce.* We export produce and manufactures of the value of £6 3s. 2d. per head of our population. France exports at the rate of £2 18s. 8d. Our trade doubled in the fifteen years 1855–1870. The exports and imports in 1870 amounted to £547,000,000. The progress has been well sustained through the period of depression, from

Progress of British Commerce.

which we have not yet by any means emerged. In 1876 the total amount had grown to £631,000,000. Mr. Levi truly observes, in commenting on these remarkable figures, that what gives an open market to British merchandise all over the world is its universal adaptation to the wants of the populations of every climate. Luxuries are useless to the masses of mankind. Calico, iron, and hardwares are necessaries even to the least civilised peoples. The demand for these articles of universal necessity would not be supplied almost exclusively from England unless our labourers were 'really good workers.' Wages may be higher here than elsewhere. Production is cheaper, because labour is more efficient and the cost of supervision is less. The effectiveness of labour is shown by the growth of exports.

The expansion of British exports of manufactures is due to the co-operation of skilful labour with well-directed capital. The English workman may claim to share with his employer the merit due to that combination of cheapness of cost with excellence of quality, which has secured for us the pre-eminence we enjoy in the export trade of the world. Grave faults are imputed to our working classes, and their conduct in many instances may deserve censure. But, when we look abroad, we hear exactly the same complaints under similar circumstances. For information on the relations between labour and capital in foreign countries I would refer more especially to the admirable reports of our Secretaries of Legation and Consuls. Sir Henry Barron's report on Belgium in 1872 describes the condition of that country in a period of unexampled prosperity. A great rise in wages had taken place. The improvidence of the people was aggravated with their prosperity, and there was an actual decrease in the deposits in the savings banks. Pig-iron doubled in value in six months. The prices of labour and materials rose to such exorbitant rates as to absorb the whole profits of the trade. The zinc, glass, and woollen industries have passed through crises of equal severity.

Germany.   In Germany, during the period of universal inflation between 1871 and 1872, wages were advanced not less rapidly than in England. It was a period of immense profits all round. The production of iron was increased from 1,500,000 tons in 1871 to 2,250,000 tons in 1872. Prices of coal and pig-iron advanced 100 per cent. The rise of wages in all branches of trade was 37 per cent. over the average of former years. The prices of all the raw materials of industry were 50 per cent. higher. This great prosperity brought about no permanent improvement in the condition of the industrial classes. The cost of living was increased to such a degree that the workmen were but little better off than before, and money was more freely expended in intoxicating liquors. I must confine myself to a single example in order to show what alternations of misery and want were experienced in Germany. The case is taken from the report of Mr. Savile, Chief Clerk of the Treasury Department of the United States, and is published in a volume on

'Labour in Europe and America,' compiled by Mr. Young, Chief of the Bureau of Statistics of the United States. Mr. Savile describes how, at Chemnitz, a great manufacturing centre, the advance of wages from 1870 to 1872 was accompanied by a still greater advance in the cost of living. When the commercial reaction ensued wages fell 25 per cent. There was no corresponding fall in the price of food. Widespread misery was the inevitable consequence. The meagre dietary of the people did not include meat more than once a week. A few touches will sometimes produce the most striking effect in a picture. An audience of English workmen will probably appreciate the low standard of living to which the people had been reduced, when it is mentioned that Mr. Savile refers in hopeful terms to the establishment of a market at Chemnitz for the sale of horse-flesh, which, being comparatively cheap, gave them more for their money, or enabled them to get meat oftener than formerly.

In the large towns of Germany there is a widespread though morbid spirit of disaffection to the political and the social organisation under which they live. The Socialist agitation is described as a purely negative opposition to the existing order of things, and to every proposal of reform. It opposes popular education, and it is indifferent to political progress. The only exception to this negative policy is the tendency to encourage strikes.

It is not necessary to insist at greater length on the existence of troubles elsewhere. The burden we have to bear is not lightened because a heavier load is imposed on others. We may therefore proceed to examine the statement, so often repeated, that labour is dearer in England than on the Continent.

Belgium.   It is assumed that, because the scale of wages is higher, there is a corresponding difference in the net cost of production. Low wages do not necessarily imply cheap production. Certain branches of trade in Belgium have been already adverted to, and yet in Belgium the wages of the mill operatives have been reduced so low as scarcely to cover the cost of subsistence in cheap seasons, and to leave the workman with an inevitable deficit in dear seasons. Not more than 40,000 workmen in the whole country have accounts at the savings banks.

In those trades where we are exposed to foreign competition, the English workman has, in the main, performed an amount of work fully proportionate to the difference of wages in his favour ; and the fact that we are running a close race in some branches of trade with a country where higher wages prevail than those earned in England is a proof that the cost of labour is not correlative with the scale of wages.

A recent return of the import duties levied on articles of British produce shows conclusively that foreign producers, notwithstanding the nominal cheapness of labour abroad, are themselves unable to compete in the open market with our own manufacturers :

Articles	Russia	Germany	Belgium	France	United States
	Per cent.	Per cent.	Per cent.	Per cent.	Per cent.
Cotton yarns	38	7	7 to 19	—	75
Jute (sacking and canvas)	10	5	10	11 to 26	30 to 40
IRON.					
Pig . .	17	free	7	27	42
Bar . .	50	—	5	35	67 to 100
Rails for Railways . .	28	—	5	35 to 50	46 to 83

And now let us compare wages. In the United States, Mr. Lowthian Bell, in his report on the iron exhibits at the Philadelphia Exhibition, gives the following table of daily wages as the result of many inquiries in 1874 :

Wages in United States.

TRADES	UNITED STATES			NORTH OF ENGLAND
	Highest	Lowest	Average	Good men
	s. d.	s. d.	s. d.	s. d.
Carpenters . . .	12 3	5 7	9 0	5 0
Smiths	13 2	6 2	9 5	6 0
Bricklayers . . .	18 10	7 6	12 3	5 6
Machinists . . .	11 3	7 6	8 3	5 10
Enginemen . . .	—	—	6 6	5 6

In America, as in England, it will be observed that the building trades are disproportionately paid. The reason is the same in both cases : the demand is essentially local. Wages are given which could not be sustained if the price could be determined upon a balance of demand and supply distributed over a wider area. In all trades, subject in any degree to the influence of foreign competition, the American workmen are conscious of the necessity of working hard and well, in order to keep up the high wages which they are at present earning. I do not shrink from telling the representatives of English labour whom I see before me, that any rules and regulations whereby the native vigour of the British workman is restrained must in the end prove fatal in their consequences. No doubt the effects are less baneful, in a commercial point of view, in the building and other trades, which are not brought face to face with foreign competitors. But, if improved dwellings are urgently needed for the working classes, the unwisdom of imposing rules and restrictions, tending to augment the cost of building, must be patent to all.

American miners.

These remarks may be enforced by a reference to Mr. Lowthian Bell's comparison, made in 1874, of the net cost of labour in the coal mines in the United States and England. The American miners earned on the average 9s. a day. They worked for ten hours, and extracted six tons of coal. The average earnings of the English miners were 5s. 2d. a day, spending about seven hours in the pit and six in actual work. This was equal to 1s. 2d. per hour, for which the quantity worked was about 11 cwt. Miners in the United States got about 13 cwt., and were paid 1s. 1d. an hour. It is admitted that this comparison is not complete, unless the relative facility of extraction is taken into consideration. The work is generally easier in America than in England. Still the fact remains that, while the

daily earnings in America were greater, the hours
were longer, and more work was done for a given
sum of money.

Provided the necessity of keeping down the cost, Chemnitz
so as to be able to compete with other producers, is
duly recognised, and the cost of living is not raised
to such a point that the workmen are actually
poorer than before, as in the case already quoted
of the manufacturing population of Chemnitz, the
working classes are clearly justified in seeking to
better their condition. If they prefer to shorten
the hours of work they are not more deserving of
reproach than the successful employer who wisely
prefers to give less time to business and more to
nobler things. In either case it is a question of
fitness of opportunity.

Apathetic resignation is a condition very detri-
mental to the interests of capital, and truly melancholy to the labourer. In Mr. Young's volume the
manufacturing population of Silesia is described as
destitute of any aspiration to better their condition
in life, while the monotony of their daily toil produces an inordinate longing for enjoyment. The
United States Consul thus describes the people
of Chemnitz : 'A stupid nature and dull ambition,
with the inborn idea that they will labour all their
lives, as their fathers did before them, make the
working class of some portions of Germany perpetual
slaves to poverty, and the day is very far off when
they shall be emancipated from thraldom.' It is
because it is so important to inspire workmen with
the hope of bettering their condition that I have

always advocated the principle of payment by results. My father entertained the firmest convictions on this point. Many trades unions object on the ground that payment by the piece leads to overwork and bad workmanship. Whatever the form of payment, whether it be by piece-work, contract, gratuity for extra diligence, or percentage upon profits, it is essentially necessary to give to the workman a personal motive for exertion. This must come from the prospect of participation in the profits which have been earned by his labour.

Rate of interest in England.

That profits on the average are not immoderate the workers in England have conclusive proof. Take the dividends paid on railways. The share and loan capital of the railways of the United Kingdom forms an enormous total of £630,000,000. The average amount of dividend or interest returned for 1875 is represented by the modest figure of 4.54 per cent. The rates of interest on preferential capital, being more uniform than the dividends on ordinary shares, afford the most accurate gauge of the ordinary returns on English investment, which present no speculative features. The process of converting terminable loans into debenture stock has of late been going forward with rapid strides. The amount increased from £67,000,000 in 1831 to £123,000,000 in 1875. In the same period the rate of interest on these investments was reduced from 4.25 to 4.18 per cent. The fact that debenture stocks, bearing only 4 per cent. interest, can be issued by our railway companies, at the rate of £16,000,000 a year, must be a positive proof to the working classes that they are not overcharged for the use of capital.

This fact might be established upon evidence of a still wider and more conclusive kind than that afforded by the prices of railway securities. We might refer, for example, to the average Bank rate of discount. The rate for each year since 1867 has been as follows :—$2\frac{1}{2}$, $2\frac{1}{4}$, $3\frac{1}{4}$, $3\frac{1}{8}$, $2\frac{7}{8}$, $4\frac{7}{8}$, $4\frac{3}{4}$, $3\frac{3}{4}$, $3\frac{1}{4}$, and $2\frac{5}{8}$ per cent. If the secure profits of business had been greatly in excess of the Bank rates, there would have been less money on deposit, and higher rates would have been charged for banking accommodation.

No less than 75,000 miles of railway have been constructed in the United States. A large proportion of the capital required has been raised in Germany and the United Kingdom upon terms more favourable to the capitalist than are obtainable here. Setting aside the speculative stocks, the rates of interest obtainable in the United States, as com pared with the United Kingdom, on a first-rate security, may be taken to be as 6 to 4. Fortunately for the English workman, there are some considerations apart from the rate of interest which make in his favour. If these did not exist, the depletion of capital in this country would become a very serious question.

Demand and supply regulate wages.

I have spoken of the faults of the workmen. In fairness I am bound to say that the present depression of trade cannot be wholly laid to their charge. If we examine the recent labour movement, in order of time the inflation of trade preceded the inflation

H

of wages. When the labourer had gained command
of the situation, he in many instances gave a smaller
return, both in quantity and quality of work, for
the increased wages that were earned. The capitalist, however, must bear his share of responsibility.
Capitalists, employers of labour, investors and
lenders of money, overstock markets and cause
goods to be sold at ruinous prices, and by encouraging speculative building temporarily raise
wages.

For the sake of brevity, it will be necessary
to confine ourselves almost exclusively to an examination of the recent history of the iron trade.
Iron trade in America. In America the panic in the iron trade began to
manifest its approach in 1873. Mr. Lowthian Bell
tells us that the ironmasters complain that the
construction of railways had been encouraged, in
the period more immediately preceding the panic,
by the action of Congress. Millions of acres of
public lands had been given to the companies, as
an inducement to make railroads which were not
needed. Upon this there supervened a disastrous
crisis. The unduly rapid extension of railways
caused an excessive demand for rails. The supply not
being equal to the demand, and a heavy protective
tariff being imposed on imported rails, the American
ironmasters realised immense profits. They rapidly
increased the rolling capacity of their mills to an
extent not warranted by the permanent prospects
of trade. The consumption of rails in 1872 was
1,530,000 tons, of which 1,000,000 tons were made
in America. In 1875 the capacity of the rail mills

had been augmented to 1,940,000 tons. In the interval, however, a panic in railways had reduced the consumption of rails to 810,000 tons. The capacity of the mills had been increased to two and a half times the requirements. A collapse ensued, from which there is no immediate prospect of recovery.

The experiences of the American ironmasters were repeated in the contemporary history of the British iron trade, though the fluctuations were less violent. The course of events is succinctly narrated in Mr. Lowthian Bell's report. The increased demand for coal and iron commenced in 1871. The increase amounted to 6½ per cent. for coal and 22 per cent. for iron. In pig-iron there was an increased production of 664,000 tons in 1871, and of 110,000 tons in 1872 ; the totals being for 1870—coals, 117,000,000 tons ; pig-iron, 6,627,000 tons. The supply was still deficient. Pig-iron rose to 122s. 6d. in August 1872. In 1873 the average price of 115s. was maintained throughout the year. The production fell off to the extent of 175,000 tons. The difficulty of obtaining fuel was the cause of diminution. Coke, which could be had for 12s. in 1870, rose to 42s. a ton in 1873. British consumers were obliged to compete, as purchasers of fuel, with foreign consumers. Meanwhile labour rose at the blast furnaces 50 per cent. The cost of production was increased fully one-third. In 1874 the reaction set in rapidly. Cleveland pig-iron receded from 115s. to 67s. 6d. In 1875 the price fell to 54s., the average for the year being

British iron trade.

60*s*. By this time a considerable economy had been effected in the cost of the manufacture, and there was a small margin of profit. In 1876 there was a further reduction of wages, and if the trade was nevertheless unprofitable it was due to causes independent of the cost of labour. To an un-biassed mind this brief retrospective narrative will scarcely support the assumption that the violent dislocations which have occurred were attributable to the action of the workmen.

Joint-stock companies. Again, the manufacturing industry of the country, especially in coal and iron, has been injured by the abuse of the facilities afforded by the Joint-Stock Companies Acts for the conversion of private into corporate enterprises. Mr. Gladstone has de-nounced in telling language the folly of investors, who deluded themselves with the belief that they could expect, as shareholders in a company, to reap all the profits which had before been earned by trained and experienced manufacturers, who had spent their early lives in learning, and their maturer years in the administration of, a complicated industry. In most cases the companies, on taking over the business from the vendors, expended large sums in additional plant and buildings. In order to find employment for their enlarged establish-ments, contracts were taken with no regard to price. The administration was often entrusted to directors without technical or practical knowledge, who could not know whether the tenders they were submitting were based on sound calculations.

This discussion of the labour problem must be

brought to a close with a few general remarks on Trades Unions. It has been asserted by Sir Edmund Beckett, who gives expression to views very widely entertained, (1) that trades unions are a combination to do less work for the given wages ; (2) that they teach the fatal doctrine that it is the business of working men to do no more than the least they can be paid for.

These grave charges may be true in a measure. They are not the whole truth. If it be true that bad workmanship is advocated by trades unions, it must at least be admitted that the national reputation is still high for the production of many important articles of a quality far superior to that obtained abroad. In textile industry the quality of our woollens, prices being taken into consideration, is unrivalled. In ship-building, machinery, and hardware we have an admitted superiority. We are practically monopolists of the unsubsidised traffic through the Suez Canal.

The existence of trades unions must be accepted as a necessary consequence of the new phases into which productive industry has entered ; and the only practical question is, how to direct this important and extensive organisation into a useful channel. The working classes must always be more or less in a state of uncertainty as to the profits which their employers may from time to time be realising. This must, however, be known, in order to decide whether they have a right to demand an advance of wages, or, what is the same thing, a reduction in the hours of labour. The organisation

Trades unions.

of the trades unions may be usefully employed for the purpose of obtaining reliable information from independent sources, both at home and abroad. As a practical suggestion, I venture to add, do not grudge an ample salary to a competent adviser. The action of the trades unions need not be confined to the single question of wages. You have shown in the present Congress that you appreciate your responsibilities in the watchful observation of legislative measures affecting the welfare of the people. You may act as peacemakers in the negotiation of terms of agreement between masters and men ; you may use your influence in securing the observance of the conditions of a treaty, or acquiescence in the decrees of courts of arbitration.

Let me conclude by expressing once more my gratitude for your kind invitation to be present at this Congress. To possess your confidence is an honour of which I am very sensible. It is the most regrettable incident of the organisation of industry on a large scale that the personal relations between employers and their workmen have become less intimate than before. In my own case the discontinuance of my father's business has deprived me of opportunities, which I should have greatly prized, of associating with the working class. Many prejudices may be removed by an honest interchange of ideas, face to face, in a spirit of conciliation, and with a mutual and sincere desire to reach the truth and to maintain justice.

CHAPTER VII

LABOUR AT HOME AND ABROAD

Lecture at the Central Hall, Leicester, October 1877

HAVING discussed Trades Unionism on two previous occasions during the present Congress, I shall confine myself this evening to other subjects, which may probably be interesting to an audience composed of the representatives of the great trades of the country.

English navvies in France.

The industrial classes in England still retain many advantages, in regard to their standard of living, over the operatives of continental Europe. The physical condition of a large portion of the French population has not materially changed during the last twenty-five years. It is stated in Lord Brabazon's report that there are nine million families in France, of whom one million are in easy circumstances. The inhabitants of towns in France constitute about two-fifths, in England four-fifths of the entire population. The food of the French workman is inferior to that to which the Englishman is accustomed. In Rouen and many other manufacturing towns the dwellings of the labouring classes are wretched. The condition of the female weavers of France is thus described by Monsieur Jules Simon : 'They are miserably lodged, clothed, and fed ; and with all this they are obliged to work twelve hours a day.'

Wages in France.

In Belgium, again, where wages are extremely low, the working classes are as a consequence wanting in strength and vigour. The employer would secure a more advantageous return for the money expended on labour if the workmen were more liberally paid. Mr. Grattan, the British Consul at Antwerp, gives a melancholy description of the condition of the working classes of Belgium. ' The standard of wages,' he says, ' taking all things into consideration, is undoubtedly insufficient to satisfy the legitimate wants of the working population.' The average wages of mill operatives do not exceed 1s. 8d. a day. ' The working days will hardly exceed 250 in the year, making a maximum earning of £20 in a year, or about 8s. a week. Adding, in the case of the married operative, with a wife and three children, 10d. a day, earned by some member of the family, a weekly amount of 14s. will possibly be realised. The expenses of the family, calculated at the lowest possible rate, in ordinary seasons, fully absorb the earnings. In dear seasons the expenditure will exceed the earnings by at least 4s. a week. Beer, meat, and sugar are not included in the dietary. Diminish the family by one child, or add one-third to the wages of the operative, and it still remains next to impossible to make both ends meet. There are probably from ten to twenty thousand working men's households in Belgium in this sad position.' This description sufficiently proves that the wages of many trades in Belgium have been reduced to the minimum required for the meagre subsistence of the people. Nor has the industry of Belgium escaped the depression experienced elsewhere. To minimise wages is not the most effectual method of securing economy of production. It is a cheaper and a happier rule to give a fair day's wages for a fair day's work. I forbear to touch upon the social aspect of the subject. The prosperity of trade must be a thing little to be desired if it could only be attained at the price of misery and destitution.

The last report by Captain Tyler on the railways of the British Empire throws some light on the relations between wages and the cost of production in this country. While the wages of all classes of workmen employed in the construction of railways have advanced, the average cost per mile of railway open has remained for many years approximately the same—£34,099 in 1858 ;   £34,100 in 1870 ; £38,000 in 1875. As Captain Tyler remarks, the more recent railways have, with the exception of the Metropolitan and some others, been constructed at a much lower rate of cost per mile than the figure of £34,000 given as the average from 1858 to 1870.   The pressure of the higher price of labour has stimulated in the utmost degree the contriving and organising faculties of employers. More machinery has been used, an ever-widening experience has suggested more effective and econo-mical methods of work. Profits have been reduced to a minimum.

Cost of English Railways

Turn to foreign countries. In the iron trade the state of affairs in Germany and Belgium—countries of low wages—is most unsatisfactory. In France the railway iron trade is dull, Creuzot being described as almost deserted.

Depression has been severe in the coal trade. No blame attaches to the workers. In 1876, according to the circular of Messrs. Fallows, operatives worked steadily throughout the year. Colliers' wages had fallen 12½ per cent.; the market value of coal had fallen at least 20 per cent.

The reduction in prices in the coal and iron trades may be appreciated from the following figures :

	1872–3	1876
Common engine-coal at pit	7s. 6d.	2s. 6d.
Ordinary pig-iron at works	£6 to £7	£2 5s. to £3
Staffordshire bars	£16	£8
Best Bessemer rails ..	£16 10s.	£6 15s.

The profits derived from the inflated prices just quoted gave sudden and colossal fortunes to the employers and unexampled wages to the workmen. The cost of production speedily exhausted the spending power of the consumers. Numbers of furnaces are standing idle.

British trade has suffered at least as much from reckless competition as from exorbitant wages. A considerable proportion of the profits of the employers in the iron and coal trades was applied to the sinking of new pits and the extension of works, which have ever since remained but partly employed, the capital invested having thus been wholly unproductive.

Over-production.

All the foreign markets have been overstocked with British goods. In order to encourage sales in a glutted market, prices are reduced. To cover the reduction in prices, manufacturers exercise their ingenuity to produce a showy article of inferior quality. The reputation of British goods in China has been almost ruined by the use of size to give a fictitious appearance to cotton goods. Sir Brooke Robertson, the British Consul at Canton, in a recent report, has pointed out in the most forcible language the necessity for restoring the character of British industry in the East by an abandonment of these practices.

I have pointed out how the returns upon capital *Foreign invest- ments.* have been diminished at least as much by rash speculation as by the aggression of trades unions. The contractors for loans to foreign States not entitled to financial credit have worked the London Stock Exchange until the supply has at length been exhausted. The misplaced confidence of the public has been destroyed by the revelations of the Committee appointed to investigate the subject. A field no doubt there is for the reproductive employment of the savings of the Old World in the development of the resources of the New. Many a brave and laborious settler in the Far West of North America, or in the wilds of Australia, could convert to profitable use a well-timed loan of £100 from the unemployed deposits in the custody of the London bankers. But how are you to bring together the lender and the borrower ?

There must obviously be more prudence in *Short time.* the application of capital. The exaggerated profits of 1871 cannot be revived. It has been proposed by the trades unions that the depreciation of prices should be arrested by a limitation of supply,

and that the mill operatives should work short time.
Such a suggestion must be received with extreme
caution, lest, by making production more costly,
you raise the price of British goods in the neutral
markets to such a point that you are undersold by
the foreign manufacturer. Again, if, by restricting
its use, you prevent the money invested in costly
machinery from being reproductive, the result must
be that capital will be diverted from manufacturing
to other branches of business where a more satisfactory return can be obtained. There are cases
in which it is the wisest course, in the interest alike
of capital and labour, to compensate for low profits
by selling a greater quantity of the commodity.
In other cases of overtrading, the appropriate remedy
is a temporary limitation of production. There are
no abstract rules for all the varied contingencies
which may arise in the industrial world. Each case
must be dealt with according to circumstances.
It is equally the duty of the workman and of his
employer to watch closely and continuously the
course of events, with a view to select a fitting
opportunity for the advancement of prices or the
improvement of wages. Every alteration, whether
of prices or wages, is a question of expediency and
opportunity.

Conditions under which wages may be raised.

In all classes an advance of wages must be made
subject to two conditions. The cost of English
labour must not be permitted to exceed the cost of
foreign labour, nor the scale of prices be raised
beyond the capacity of the consumer to bear them.
On the other hand, if the working men offered no

resistance to the downward pressure, the reduction would continue until wages had been reduced to the minimum required to cover the cost of subsistence. The employers would reap no benefit. Keen competition would give everything to the consumer. If labour were cheaper in England than it is, the workman would share with the whole body of consumers the advantages of a reduction in the cost of living, which would go far to compensate for the reduction of wages.

Much of the objection which exists in the public mind to trades unions rests on general reluctance to see any effort made to raise the price of labour ; but if it be inexpedient to seek for an advance of wages, all those requirements or prejudices which make the cost of living of the working classes dearer in this country than on the Continent may with equal justice be condemned. The British workman has a prejudice against brown bread, and insists on eating white bread. If he were content with brown bread, he would live more cheaply. But what is the effect of this prejudice ? It is that the British workman will prefer to labour more and live on white bread, rather than labour less and live on brown bread. It is needless to give further details in illustration. All political economists are agreed that a high standard of living is an encouragement to industry, and that a low standard of living tends to indolence. A demand for higher wages is only the aspiration to a higher standard of living in another form ; and, provided that it be recognised that for the higher wages an equivalent must be

Cost of living in England.

given in better work and more work, there can be
no objection to the demand. A rise in wages,
without an equivalent increase in work performed,
is only possible where there is a margin of profit
available for division among the workmen. It is
the business of trades unions to gather materials
for forming a judgment as to whether such a margin
exists. Where it does not exist, and the workman
knows that he must do more work or better work
in order to secure an advance of wages, the aspiration
for a higher standard of living is distinctly beneficial
both to capital and labour.

Workmen
in the
United
States.
I pass from the abstract rules of political economy
to the practical results of high wages, as exhibited
in the social condition of the industrial population of
the United States. During the period of prosperity
anterior to the recent collapse of trade in the United
States, there is reason to believe that the working
man in America, like his fellow-labourer in England,
spent nearly the whole of his earnings on the main-
tenance of his family and household. If, however,
his savings were not appreciably greater, his standard
of living was much higher than that of the corresponding classes in our own country. In New York
the dwellings of the workmen were often crowded
to excess, and the same remark is applicable to some
of the towns of New England. For the most part,
the working people of the United States inhabited
comfortable houses and enjoyed an abundance of
good food and clothing. Their children enjoyed
the advantage of an admirable system of public
elementary education. The circumstances of eighty-

one workmen, including carpenters, masons, shoe-makers, and mill hands, were examined by the Bureau of Statistics in the State of Massachusetts in 1874. The results are given as follows:

EXPENDITURE

Rent	$146 58
Fuel	51 19
Groceries	350 38
Meat and fish	108 28
Milk	25 47
Clothing, boots and shoes .	114 65
Dry goods	28 27
Religion and books . . .	23 18
Sundries	38 76
Total	$886 76 @ 4s. 2d. = £184

The earnings were as follows:

The father	$619 18
The children	310 78
Total	$929 96 @ 4s. 2d. = £195
Number of rooms occupied . . .	5
Persons in family	6
Children at school	2

Five houses were reported as unpleasant in situation, eight were moderately, the rest well furnished, thirteen contained pianos, and three had organs. All the families save three were 'well dressed.' Yet, with all these comforts, not to say luxuries, only sixteen had deposited money in savings banks.

The advantages enjoyed by the working classes

in the United States are seriously diminished by the protective policy of the country. The trade is confined to the home market ; and the fluctuations must be more frequent and more violent than in a country which has commercial relations with the whole world. In the case of a country which has a large export trade, the demand for goods, if dull in one market, will probably be brisk in another. Under a free-trade policy employment will accordingly be more regular. No condition can be more trying to the working classes than the alternation of high wages and certain employment with intervals of complete inactivity. We have had much experience of this evil in England. It is aggravated in America by the existence of the protective tariff, which makes manufactures so dear as to render exportation impossible.

The depression of trade in the United States has brought more suffering on the working classes in that country than the English operatives have endured, although I fully recognise the claims of our fellow-countrymen to our sympathy. This is shown by the reports received from my old friend Mr. Thomas Connolly. In a letter, republished in the *Economist*, he says that in Pennsylvania, which has a population of $3\frac{1}{2}$ millions, there are more people out of work than in all England. A few individual cases may be quoted. A steel-roller at Distin's saw factory, who came out from Sheffield at 7 dollars a day, is now working, two days a week, at $3\frac{1}{2}$ dollars a day. The men on the Delaware and Western Railroad had to submit to three reductions in 1876, which brought down the wages of good workmen to 4s. 10d. a day. The only emigrants who are now required in the United States are agricultural labourers and men who can buy land and settle on it.

The most serious difficulties of the working classes in England arise from :

1. Overcrowding in our densely peopled cities.

2. An excessive supply of labour in certain industries.

The gifted author of ' The New Republic ' has described the unlovely conditions in which the dwellers in great cities are in too many cases compelled to exist. 'Consider,' he asks, 'how the human eye delights in form and colour, and the ear is tempered to harmonious sounds ; and then think for a moment of a London street—think of the shapeless houses, the forest of ghastly chimney pots ! '

We may look for improved conditions under the provisions of the Industrial Dwellings Act, carried through Parliament by the Home Secretary, at the instance of my friend and colleague, Sir Ughtred J. Kay-Shuttleworth.

I cannot bring these remarks to a conclusion without expressing my deep satisfaction that many men and women, some young in years and great favourites in high society, with every temptation to live a life of pleasure, devote night after night to the organisation of workmen's clubs, to the furtherance of the co-operative movement. There are earnest advocates of your cause in classes of society which have no practical knowledge of your aims and objects or of your condition of life.

The vindication of the rights of property, and the scientific explanation of the causes of the accumulation of wealth in some fortunate individuals, are themes I cannot now discuss. To the wise man riches are a weighty responsibility, and to the weak man a sore temptation. While the follies of the one are contemptible, the anxieties of the other may sometimes deserve the sympathy of the independent artisan. Far as they are apart, the various classes of society depend on one another. In their union consists our national strength and individual happiness. It was to promote that union that I came among you, and I go away with many grateful memories of my visit to Leicester.

CHAPTER VIII

ON THE RISE OF WAGES IN THE BUILDING TRADES OF LONDON

Read before the Royal Institute of British Architects, February 4, 1878

THE present Paper has been prepared in compliance with an invitation of long standing, which I esteem it a great honour to have received. The delay in the preparation of the following statement is due to the pressure of many engagements, and to my protracted absence on a voyage of circumnavigation. Even now I should have been quite unable to have performed my task without the aid and co-operation of others. I have little spare time for such an investigation, and no technical knowledge. Under these circumstances I applied to Messrs. Hunt and Stephenson, the well-known surveyors. As representatives of the builders, I communicated with my old friends, Messrs. Lucas Brothers; and lastly, with a view to obtain a fair statement on behalf of the workmen, I asked the co-operation of Mr. Howell. If the following paper possesses any importance as a contribution to the sum of knowledge on that labour movement which constitutes one of the most urgent questions of our time, it is to the practical authorities whom I have quoted that its value must be attributed.

To the Council of this Institute belongs the credit of suggesting that a review of the alterations in the rates of wages in the building trades should be prepared. It is only by bringing into view the fluctuations in prices during a tolerably extended period that the relation between cause and effect can be satisfactorily traced, and principles laid down for the future guidance of masters and men. It was truly said by Lord Bolingbroke, that 'history is philosophy teaching us by examples how to conduct ourselves in all the struggles of public and private life.'

I begin by giving a statement of the increase of wages and reduction of working hours in the building trades in London from 1837 to 1847. The current wages of building operatives in London from the year 1836 were 5s. per day of ten hours, or 30s. per week of sixty hours. This rate was generally adopted, though not universally paid in all branches of the building trades until 1847. In fact, it was only established as the standard rate by dint of protracted efforts, extending over a period of several years. Masons and bricklayers were the first to secure an advance. Carpenters, plasterers, and painters followed.

Surveying a period of 30 years, there has been a reduction since 1847 of 7½ hours in time—that is to say, from 60 hours per week to 52½ hours. The current wages in 1847 were at the rate of 5s. per day of 10 hours, or 30s. per week for 60 hours' work. In 1877 the current wages were £1 12s. 4½d. for 52½ hours' work, being an increase of wages amounting to 9s. 4½d. per week. This represents a rise of

$31\frac{1}{2}$ per cent. on the original scale of wages, at the rate of 30s. per week, and of $12\frac{1}{2}$ per cent. in time value, or a total advance in 30 years of 44 per cent.

Messrs. Lucas have prepared a memorandum giving the various wages by the day or the hour both for labourers and mechanics. It will be seen upon examination that these figures, although stated in a different form, correspond exactly with those contained in Mr. Howell's Paper:

Memorandum of the Cost of Materials and Labour, &c., in the Building Trades

—	Mechanics	Labourers
Sept. 1853. Wages per day of 10 hours = 60 hours per week were	5 0	3 0
Sept. 4, 1853, to March 22, 1861. Wages per day of 10 hours=60 hours per week were	5 6	3 4
March 23, 1861, to Sept. 27, 1865. Payment by the day was discontinued, and the men were paid at the rate per hour of	0 7	0 $4\frac{1}{4}$
Sept. 28, 1865, to May 4, 1866. Ditto	0 $7\frac{1}{2}$	0 $4\frac{1}{2}$
May 5, 1866, to July 5, 1872. ,,	0 8	0 $4\frac{3}{4}$
July 6, 1872, to Aug. 1, 1873. ,,	0 $8\frac{1}{2}$	0 $5\frac{1}{4}$
Aug. 2, 1873, to present time. ,,	0 9	0 $5\frac{3}{4}$

The present Working Hours are:

Monday	9 hours
Tuesday	$9\frac{1}{2}$,,
Wednesday	$9\frac{1}{2}$,,
Thursday	$9\frac{1}{2}$,,
Friday	$9\frac{1}{2}$,,
Saturday	$5\frac{1}{2}$,,
Total	$52\frac{1}{2}$ hours

as compared with 60 hours for the summer and 47 hours for the winter season, commencing six weeks before and ending six weeks after Christmas.

This shows an increase of 50 per cent. in the wages of mechanics, and 64 per cent. in those of labourers. There is a loss in time of $7\frac{1}{2}$ hours per week. The men now only work $52\frac{1}{2}$ instead of 60 hours—a reduction of $12\frac{1}{2}$ per cent. in time; mechanics receive 39s. $4\frac{1}{2}d$. for the $52\frac{1}{2}$ hours, instead of 30s. for 60 hours; the labourers also work $12\frac{1}{2}$ per cent. less time and receive 25s. 2d. for $52\frac{1}{2}$ hours as against 18s. for 60 hours.

It is a remarkable circumstance that the most important advances have been obtained by the unskilled workmen. The lower the original rate of wage the greater has been the advance. This is clearly shown in the following table prepared by Mr. Stephenson:

Memorandum with reference to the Comparative Cost of Wages and Materials for Builders' Works in 1865 and 1875

Wages	In 1865 per hour	In 1875 per hour	Increase
	d.	d.	
Excavators . . .	$4\frac{3}{4}$	$6\frac{1}{4}$	28 per cent.
Bricklayers . . .	$7\frac{1}{2}$	9	20 ,,
Masons	$7\frac{1}{2}$	9	20 ,,
,, Fixers . .	8	$9\frac{1}{2}$	20 ,,
Carpenters . . .	$7\frac{1}{2}$	9	20 ,,
Joiners	$7\frac{1}{2}$	9	20 ,,
Smiths	$7\frac{1}{2}$	9	20 ,,
Plasterers . . .	$7\frac{1}{2}$	9	20 ,,
Painters and Glaziers .	7	$8\frac{1}{2}$	22 ,,
Plumbers . . .	$8\frac{1}{2}$	10	$17\frac{1}{2}$,,
General Labourers .	$4\frac{1}{4}$	$5\frac{3}{4}$	35 ,,
Scaffolders . . .	$4\frac{3}{4}$	$6\frac{1}{4}$	28 ,,
Plumbers' Labourers .	$4\frac{3}{4}$	$6\frac{1}{4}$	28 ,,

It might have been expected that in trades where the Unions were most completely organised the greatest advances would have been secured. This has not happened. While the number of the unskilled labourers is not limited by any necessity for a preliminary apprenticeship, it is they who have reaped the greatest benefit by the increased demand for labour. The rise in the rate of wages is doubtless due partly to the increased cost of living. The pay of those labourers whose wages were nearest to a mere subsistence-level has been most sensibly influenced by the changes which have led to an increase in the cost of articles of the first necessity.

Let us now ascertain how far the cost of building has been influenced by the increased cost of labour. First, as to the cost of materials. Messrs. Lucas observe ' The cost of materials fluctuates from time to time, but as a whole we find that the average cost is about the same as formerly, the reduction of duty on bricks, timber, glass, &c., being in our favour.'

The increase of wages, according to Messrs. Lucas, ought to have been more than covered by the introduction of machinery for many building operations, for hoisting all materials instead of carrying by hod and raising by hand labour ; for grinding mortar and for the execution of all kinds of carpenter's, joiner's, and mason's work. They say, however, that their experience shows that the cost of building has actually increased from 20 to 30 per cent., and this increase is entirely due to the small amount of work now done by the men, compared with what they did some few years ago.

As an illustration of this, they refer to the new station, hotel, locomotive works, and goods' sheds at York, which they have recently erected for the North Eastern Railway Company. These works were of great magnitude, and were superintended by one of the most experienced and able members of their staff. The materials were bought for less than the estimated price, and the introduction of steam-power to an unusual extent—in fact, whenever it could be used—effected an immense saving upon the labour. But all these advantages were more than neutralised by the indolence of the men. A conspicuous instance is quoted. The labour upon the brickwork, which would formerly have cost 38s. per rod by piece-work, was estimated at a price which Mr. Harrison, the Engineer of the North Eastern Railway Company, considered liberal for such work, namely, £3 3s. per rod. The actual cost was a little more than £5 or £1 17s. per rod more than Messrs. Lucas received from the Company. In this case, therefore, a loss of 55 per cent. was sustained upon the estimate for labour. If, however, the men had done a fair and proper amount of work the cost would have been as follows:

	£	s.	d.	
With wages at the price formerly paid, at the rate of 6d. per hour . .	1	18	0	per rod
Add 50 per cent. for increase of wages at present time	0	19	0	,,
	2	17	0	,,

In point of fact, the actual cost, as before stated, was a little over 100s. per rod, and this notwithstanding all the additional advantage of the possession of steam-power. This illustration proves beyond all doubt that the men at the present time do very little more than half the work for 9d. per hour that they formerly did for 6d.

These experiences of a large building firm are corroborated from a different and perhaps a more impartial point of view by Messrs. Hunt and Stephenson. An opportunity of applying an accurate test to determine the depreciation or appreciation in the cost of buildings has recently occurred, Mr. Stephenson having been called upon to make a close professional estimate of the cost of re-erecting an ordinary dwelling-house which had been built in 1865 for the sum of £5000. The building in question was demolished to make room for a Metropolitan Railway Extension. It would cost £5624 to rebuild it in 1875. The following are some details as calculated by Mr. Stephenson :

Estimate showing the Amount of each Trade in a Building of an Assured Cost of £5000 and the Increase in Cost of both Labour and Materials.

Labour	1865 Apportioned Value of each Trade	1865 Relative proportion of Labour and Materials		1875 Increase in Cost of Labour		1875 Increase in Cost of Materials		Decrease	Proportion of Cost of Labour to Cost of Materials in the several Trades — Labour Per ct.	Plant and Materials Per ct.	Average Increase and Decrease in Total Cost in 1875 over 1865	
	£	£	£	Per cent.	£	Per cent.	£	£	Per cent.	Per cent.	£	£
Excavator . . . 90	100	90	10	28	25	—	—	—	90	10		25
Bricklayer . . . 25	1200	300	900	27	81	25	80	100	25	75	19	—
Mason . . . 60	800	480	320	24	115	20	8		60	40		195
Slater . . . 10	50	10	40	27¼	3	7	21		20	80		11
Plumber . . . 25	400	100	300	24	24	16	51		25	75		45
Joiner . . . 60	800	480	320	20	96	—	—		60	40		147
Smith and Founder. 20	350	70	280	20	14	14	37		20	80		14
Tiler . . . 25	350	88	262	25	22	10	16		25	75		59
Plasterer . . . 60	400	240	160	27	65	{20	25		60	40		81
Glazier . . . 15½	150	23	127	22}	22	5}	4		15	{85		
Painter . . . 50	150	75	75	22}					50	50}		51
		1956	2794		467		242	100			15	
					1956		100				643	
					2423		142				19	
							2794				624	
							2936				5000	
Fees of Quantity-Surveyor, Local Authorities, and Sundry other Fees, &c.	250					265					£5624	
	£5000	£5000				£5624. Nearly 12½ per cent. advance on 1865.						

Having given the results of the experience of large employers in this country, it may be interesting to you to know that the diminished industry of foreign operatives under the same conditions has been even more conspicuous. The following paragraph recently appeared in the *Times* newspaper :

'At the time when prices were most inflated the work and wages of masons in Berlin were submitted to a crucial test. Between 1868 and 1873 the wages of this class of operatives were increased by 50 per cent. In the former year a certain number of masons were accustomed to dress 618 stones of a particular description in a week. In 1873 the same number of men dressed in the same time no more than 304 stones, less than half ; and as they were paid as much for the smaller as the greater quantity, it follows that the cost of building a house in Berlin had more than doubled within a period of six years. A similar process has been going on, with more or less rapidity, in most of the cities of Germany and Switzerland. Professor Gustav Kohn, in a pamphlet recently published (*Deutsche Zeit- und Streit-Fragen. Heft 77. Vertheurung des Lebensunterhaltes in der Gegenwart. Von Gustav Kohn. Berlin, 1876*), compares the cost of building in London and Zürich, and although there is no great difference between the two places in the price of materials, he arrives at the conclusion that it costs twice as much to erect and finish a house in the Swiss city as in the metropolis of Great Britain, and to this difference he attributes the fact that rents are so much higher in the latter place than in the former. In order to arrive at a just conclusion, he eliminates from his comparison the business and fashionable quarters, where the question might be complicated by the elements of expensive sites and heavy ground rents, and chooses in the most outward periphery of the town a locality which is to Zürich what Wimbledon is to London. If the result of the Professor's investigations is to be trusted, a dwelling that at Wimbledon is rented at £40 a year could not be obtained at Zürich for less than from 1500 francs to 2000 francs a year. And as wages, the cost of materials, the value of money and of land, are approximately the same in both places, it follows that the difference in rents must arise from the superior skill of English builders and the greater efficiency of English labour. This is the conclusion of Herr Kohn, based as well on induction as on his own personal observation and inquiries.'

Mr. Howell contends that the net cost of building has not increased in proportion to the advance of wages. He points to the use of machinery in some branches, to the introduction of better appliances in others, and to the development of greater skill in special branches. As a rule, he considers that the foremen are much superior in ability and character to the majority of those who previously had charge of large undertakings. As an instance of work being done more cheaply, he refers to a statement made to him by a mason of considerable experience and skill, to the effect that each of the blocks of the fluted columns at the British Museum cost, on an average, £5, whereas now he would be glad to undertake any number of them at £3 10s. each.

This reduction in the price of stonework for the British Museum would, however, only be possible upon the piece-work system. Piece-work is earnestly desired by the masters. Messrs. Lucas remark ' By the rules and regulations of the trades unions no set-work or piece-work is allowed.

' The foregoing observations apply to architectural buildings only, and not to contracting and engineering works. These are mainly carried out upon the plan adopted by the late Mr. Brassey, that of *set-work*. A certain amount of pay is offered for a given amount of work. The men are paid for any work done in excess of the minimum amount allowed, and this is the only fair and satisfactory course to be adopted in the building trades in the interests of the men, the masters, and of the public generally.'

Having given in detail the successive advances in wages, and shown the increase in the cost of building, it will be interesting to inquire how far the condition of the operatives has been substantially improved by the rise in the rates of wages. Has there been any appreciable improvement in their food and in their dwellings ? Is their leisure time profitably and innocently employed ? Mr. Howell has supplied a complete statement on this subject. We will take first the article of meat. The rise

in the price of meat is concisely shown in the subjoined table :

Date	Average Prices					
	Beef—per stone	Increase	Per cent.	Mutton—per stone	Increase	Per cent.
	s. d.	s. d.		s. d.	s. d.	
1847–53	4 2½	—	—	4 5	—	—
1853–67	5 0½	0 10	20	5 9	1 4	30
1867–73	5 6	1 4	30	6 4	1 11	43
1874–75	5 8½	1 6	35½	6 5	2 0	45
1876–77	5 11	1 9½	39	6 9	2 5	50

In round figures, the price of meat, wholesale in
the market, has increased, in the case of beef about
40 per cent., mutton about 50 per cent. Pork has
increased proportionately, and bacon at a higher
rate still. The price obtained for beasts at the
Annual Cattle Shows from 1847 to 1877 is as follows :
From 1847 to 1856 inclusive, the average price
ranged from 4s. per stone for seconds, to 5s. 7½d.
for prime cattle. From 1857 to 1866 inclusive,
the average price ranged from 4s. 1d. for seconds,
to 6s. 2d. for prime qualities. From 1867 to 1877
inclusive, the average price ranged from 5s. 6¼d. for
seconds, to 8s. 1½d. for prime meat. During the
latter period the quality of meat has greatly improved. On the other hand, the poorer classes have
had to pay more per pound for inferior meat than the
wealthier classes have paid for joints of the best
quality. The retail price of meat to working people
has been increased not less than 75 per cent., or
oftener 80 per cent., and butchers are more careful

than formerly not to cut to waste. Hence, there are fewer pieces called 'block ornaments.' This is equally true as regards slices of bacon. Poultry and fish have advanced in price nearly, if not quite, in the same ratio as meat. Rabbits fetch even a higher price in proportion. As for hares and other game, the poorer classes seldom taste such things. They know nothing of them, except what they see at the poulterers' shops.

Take next the items of bread, vegetables, clothing, and rent. The price of British wheat has varied from 50s. 6d. per quarter in 1848 to 74s. 8d. in 1855, the highest quotation during the past thirty years. Since 1864 it has varied from 40s. 2d. to 64s. 5d. in 1867. The average prices quoted for the last five years have been : In 1873, 61s. 8d. ; 1874, 44s. 2d. ; 1875, 45s. 3d. ; 1876, 50s. 3d. ; 1877, 51s. 9d. The ordinary baker's bread in the poorer districts is now 7d. and 7½d. per 4-lb. loaf. It has not been so low as 6d. per loaf for some years. Very inferior bread is nominally cheaper, though actually it is the dearest, in proportion to the solid nourishment it contains. The prices of potatoes and other vegetables as sold at the greengrocers' shops have gone up during the past thirty years as much as 100 per cent. Potatoes, formerly sold at a half-penny per pound, and then at the rate of 3 lbs. for 2d., are now 1½d. per pound, being an increase of over 100 per cent. Cabbages, which could be bought at a halfpenny each, are now 2d. or 2½d. Turnips, formerly sold at 2d. per bunch, are now from 5d. to 6d. The price of parsnips has advanced

from a halfpenny to three halfpence ; and all other
kinds of garden produce are equally enhanced in
price.   Coal, butter, and cheese are most important
items, especially the two former.   Many thousands
of the working-classes purchase their coal by the
cwt. or in sacks.   For some years past the lowest
price charged per cwt. has been 1*s*. 6*d*. or 30*s*. per
ton.   In 1872–73 the price went up to 50*s*. per ton.
The coal consumed by the work people is generally
inferior, and the purchasers are robbed in weight
and measure.   Those who live in apartments have
seldom room for more than a sack at a time.   In
newer houses room is provided for half a ton or a ton.
The article of butter has ranged from 1*s*. 6*d*. per lb.
to 1*s*. 10*d*. for inferior qualities, described as little
better than mere grease.   The consumption of salt
butter has diminished of late years.   Brittany
butter has been substituted.   Cheese, cheap in days
gone by, is now rather a luxury.   It is not used by
poor people as it was formerly.   The only articles
on which there has been a reduction are sugar and
tea.   Most working people concur in saying that tea,
as sold at the grocers, is not so good as formerly.
House rent has greatly increased.   Apartments of
two rooms on a floor have gone up from 4*s*. 6*d*. and
5*s*. 6*d*. to 8*s*. 6*d*. and 9*s*. per week.   The rent of
single rooms has risen from 2*s*. 9*d*. and 3*s*. 6*d*. to 5*s*.
and 5*s*. 6*d*.   Small houses are scarce.   For a house
with four rooms and a wash-house the rents have
advanced from 6*s*. or 6*s*. 6*d*. to 10*s*. or 11*s*.
Peabody's Buildings and the Model Dwellings are
full to repletion.   So great is the demand for

accommodation that enough names are down on the books to fill several more blocks of houses. Boots and shoes are dearer, and the leather is not so good. These articles are of the first importance to working people, who have to work out of doors, or walk long distances. Clothing has also gone up in price, although not in the same proportion as other articles. Apparel, however, is usually bought ready-made by machinery, and as machine-sewing is inferior to hand-sewing, clothing is less durable. Cottons and flannels are cheaper, but stuffs and homespuns are dearer, at retail prices, and the quality is much depreciated. Almost every little article of domestic consumption has increased in price. Though the increase in cost may only amount to a halfpenny, the advance is often equivalent to a rise of 40 to 50 per cent. on a small item. It is the universal complaint of the wives of workmen in the present day that they have a difficulty in ' keeping house ' in consequence of the dearness of everything. The working classes obtain their supplies under peculiar disadvantages, from being obliged to buy in small quantities at hucksters' shops, or what are called ' general shops,' where they pay the best price for very inferior articles. The poorer the neighbourhood, the greater the difficulty in obtaining articles of good quality ; and yet the prices charged are very nearly equal to those charged for the best qualities in the best establishments.

The well-managed Co-operative Stores of the North of England have provided a most effective

K

means of supplying the wants of the working classes. In the metropolis co-operative organisation has been but slowly and imperfectly developed. Perhaps the very number of the population has made co-operation more difficult. Less cohesion, less interdependence, and less mutual sympathy will be found in the multitudinous masses of the metropolis than in the more compact populations of our northern cities, where similarity of employment and a more uniform social status bind the people together, and both dispose and enable them to combine more readily for a common object. Mr. Howell concludes by stating that, with all the drawbacks which he has enumerated, the majority of workmen's houses are far superior to those of the same class thirty and even twenty years ago. There is an air of comfort and cleanliness as a general rule in the homes of the artisans and mechanics, which shows progress and improvement ; and there are fewer wretched homes even in the poorest localities than of old.

I have given *in extenso* Mr. Howell's statement as to the economic condition of the operatives in the metropolis. It affords much food for reflection. It has been shown in the tables prepared by Messrs. Hunt and Stephenson, Messrs. Lucas, and Mr. Howell, that, during the period embraced in our review, wages have advanced 50 per cent. for mechanics, and 64 per cent. for labourers. In the same period, however, the cost of living has increased in such proportions that the wives of the workmen have experienced an ever-increasing difficulty in making both ends meet. Mr. Howell, indeed, describes a general improvement in the interior of the workmen's houses ; but that amelioration is probably due to advancing civilisation rather than to the increased spending power of the people. Improved taste, more refined habits, and a more restricted indulgence in intoxicating liquors would have converted a great number of the miserable hovels of thirty years ago into comfortable dwellings, even though wages had remained at the former rates. Mr. Howell's remarks as to the improvement observable in the dwellings must be understood to apply almost exclusively to the mechanics ; and we may venture to hope that the majority of the skilled workmen have made a good use of their increased wages.

The recent report of Mr. Plunkett on the railway riots in America gives most interesting details on the relation between wages and the cost of living in the United States. In America, with every advance in wages, there has been a corresponding rise of prices, while, owing to the fall in prices which has followed the recent reductions of wages, working men in regular employment have suffered no privation of the necessaries of life. Workmen are perfectly entitled to take advantage of every turn of the market in their favour. It is a delusion to suppose that a general advance in the rates of wages, accompanied as it must be by a corresponding advance in prices, is pure gain to themselves.

In connection with this subject, I must once more express my conviction that an exaggerated impression prevails of the power of the trades unions

to advance wages by the mere completeness of their
organisation, apart from other influences, which are
more effective and more natural in their operation. In every controversy with the masters the
trades unions occupy a prominent position as the
spokesmen and advocates of the workmen. The
trades unions cannot possibly force the employers
to carry on their operations at a loss, neither can
they compel the public to buy an article or to build
a house at a price which they cannot afford to pay.
The wages of mechanics in the building trades have
been rapidly raised and are now kept up solely by
the constant demand for labour in those trades.
The active prosecution of building operations seems
somewhat inconsistent with the general depression
in almost every other branch of trade. The cause of
this apparent anomaly is to be found in the failure
of joint-stock undertakings and the revelations
of the Foreign Loans Committee. Until a recent
period a large proportion of the savings of the
country were being absorbed in the conversion of
private manufacturing and trading establishments
into corporate undertakings. Large sums were
lent to weak and almost unknown Governments,
who had succeeded in alluring the too credulous
public by the offer of high rates of interest. Experience has shown that Boards of Directors, with
little personal interest in their work and no technical
knowledge, cannot take the place of an individual
manager having a large stake in the result, and
qualified by technical training and long experience
to conduct a difficult business. The joint-stock

mania has now happily subsided. It would be impossible in the present temper of the public mind to introduce on the Stock Exchange, with any prospect of success, a loan to a needy foreign State of the second rank. In the absence of other opportunities for investments, the savings of the country are now being applied to building operations. In the suburbs of the metropolis and in the environs of our provincial towns, long rows of houses are rising up built with borrowed capital. Timid people who are afraid of employing their money in more distant operations are satisfied with the security offered by a mortgage on houses erected in their own neighbourhood. They possess, in the form of a mortgage on buildings, a tangible security, and one the value of which they perfectly understand. Building has accordingly been carried on with unrelaxed energy, and possibly in excess of the wants of the public. Meanwhile, the demand for mechanics and labourers has been sustained at a time when industrial operations generally have been contracted. Thus we see a strike amongst the masons for an advance of wages at a time when the only strikes which are taking place in other trades are strikes against a reduction.

Is the present activity of the building trade likely to continue ? This is a question which well merits the attentive consideration of our workmen. Is it not an inevitable consequence of the continued depression of trade, that the savings of the country, which have lately been invested so freely in mortgages on new. buildings, must be temporarily reduced in amount ? If this be so, the demand for labour will slacken, and wages must ultimately fall. It is further to be observed that the depression of trade, so serious in this country, has been still more marked abroad. There are large multitudes of skilled men without employment on the Continent. If they are introduced into this country, the English workman has no more right to complain or to resist than the workmen in France, who quietly suffered my father to take over a body of 5000 English navvies to make the railway from Paris to Rouen. The bricks in the tunnels under the city of Rouen were all laid by London bricklayers.

It was argued at the recent conferences of the International that a general rise of wages can only be obtained by a combination among the workmen of all nations. The country in which production is dear will be driven out of the market by the production of other countries in which work is done at a cheaper rate. The same principle applies to the building as to every other trade. Hitherto, owing to the difficulty of communication, the rates of wages have been determined by local circumstances. Railways have tended to diminish these local inequalities, because the supply of labour can now be drawn from an ever-widening area. In the shipbuilding yards on the Thames the great mass of the joiners are Scotchmen, and there is but a slight difference between the wages on the Thames and on the Clyde. It is as easy to introduce masons from Hamburg as to bring joiners from Scotland. There need be no fear of the competition of foreigners with Englishmen, if only the latter will be true to themselves.   All workmen labour at a disadvantage in a foreign land.

The substitution of payment by time for payment by results is a most unfortunate innovation.   Piece-work under adequate supervision is the only system which is equitable alike to the employer, the work-man, and the public.   There can be no objection to mechanics earning 7s. or 8s. a day, provided they have fairly earned their high wages by a just amount of work.   The employer will raise no objection to the payment of liberal wages provided he knows what he will be required to pay, and how much work will be done day by day.   On the other hand, it is utterly wrong that good men and bad men should be paid at an uniform rate of 10d. per hour.   It is a system which could only have been forced upon the building trades by the unusual scarcity of labour. Such a system is only enforced by that evil spirit of jealousy, described with so much power by Dante in the 17th canto of the *Purgatorio*:

> È chi, per esser suo vicin soppresso,
>   Spera eccellenza, e sol per questo brama
>   Ch' el sia di sua grandezza in basso messo :
> È chi podere, grazia, onore, e fama
>   Teme di perder perch' altri sormonti,
>   Onde s' attrista si, che 'l contrario ama :

The passage is thus translated by Longfellow :

> There are, who, by abasement of their neighbour,
>   Hope to excel, and therefore only long
>   That from his greatness he may be cast down ;
> There are, who power, grace, honour, and renown
>   Fear they may lose because another rises,
>   Hence are so sad that the reverse they love.

The depression in trade to which I have already referred may lead to a contraction in building operations ; and it would be well that the opportunity should be embraced for setting the relations between employers and employed in the building trades on that equitable basis on which business in every other branch of trade has been conducted. No industrial organisation can be sound in which, to use the words of Mr. Herbert Spencer, 'duty done and income gained do not go hand in hand, and the failure will be great in proportion as the dependence of income upon duty is remote.'

The conclusions to be drawn from our investigation may be summed up as follows :

I. During the last thirty years there has been an increase in wages of 44 per cent., and in the cost of building of 20 to 30 per cent.

II. The advances of wages have been largely absorbed in the enhanced cost of living.

III. The increase in wages has been caused by unprecedented activity in the building trade.

IV. The prospect of a more satisfactory organisation of the building trades depends on the adoption of an equitable system of payment by piece.

I have narrated the story of the rise of wages in the building trades with strict impartiality. Many of those present regard the trades unions with a dread which I do not share. I can fully understand why it is that the trades unions are not viewed with especial favour by the master builders, who have been perpetually thwarted. It is hard to have to yield to the dictation of irresponsible men, and to be required to pay wages at rates never contemplated at the time when contracts have been entered into. I sympathise with those who have suffered many losses and vexations. If the unions connected with the building trades have given trouble, it has been the consequence of a great and sustained demand for labour. For years past no skilled mechanic in the metropolis has ever known what it is to be without employment. Our ancient and noble capital has been extended with extraordinary rapidity. Large numbers of successful men in commercial or professional careers, in the provinces or abroad, have been attracted to London, and made it year by year more and more the centre of British society in all its various grades, and a place of meeting for persons of every taste and pursuit, whether artistic, scientific, or literary. The man of pleasure and the severe student can here always find congenial companions and gratify their special tastes. It may appear that wages have been advanced under the pressure of the trades unions. Competition among the masters for labour, of which there was an insufficient supply, has been the primary cause of its enhanced value. If the demand for buildings were to abate in any sensible degree, the price of labour would fall in proportion. The instance which I have quoted at Zürich shows what advances will take place in the price of labour under the same conditions in which the London builders have been placed, and that, too, in a land of exceptionally cheap labour.

Complaints are urged of the indifference of the

trades unions to the interests of the public. No
doubt such organisations have been established to
promote the interests of a class, and not for the
general good of society. Experience of the motives
and actions of the leaders of the trades unions has
led me to believe that, although their energies are
concentrated on the single object of improving the
position of their clients, they do not seek to promote
their objects by violent measures. I attended the
late Congress of the trades unions at Leicester. I
was the only man of my own order who did attend,
and I can bear testimony to the admirable manner
in which the proceedings were conducted. The
programme of subjects for discussion was reasonable and appropriate. The questions which it was
proposed to ventilate in Parliament were fitting
topics for parliamentary debate. There was a
creditable freedom from class prejudices. Contrast
the proceedings at Leicester with the debates of
the International Society on the Continent, or the
recent demonstrations in New York, where non-
sensical declamation was applauded which would
never have been listened to in this country. Have
any of the trades unions of London ever maintained
that 'To protect the useful classes against the
avarice of capitalists, or the derangements of trade,
the various branches of useful industry should be
instituted by the Governments upon equitable
principles, and thereby furnish employment to
those who might be otherwise idle'? Has it
ever been resolved at a mass meeting in this city
'That the time has arrived for all working people

to resist by all legal means the oppression of capital and the robbery which it perpetrates on labour ' ? We have in the English working people a body of men less likely to be led away by visionary ideas, less ready to listen to vague and envious denunciations, more strongly influenced by a sense of duty and more law-abiding than the corresponding classes in any other country. With all these merits they are not exempt from human infirmity. The principle of self-interest is strong with them as it is with their masters, and it is not always enlightened. They seek to sell their labour to the highest bidder, just as the masters demand the best price which the very keen competition amongst themselves allows them to secure. I am not an advocate of a too acquiescent temper of mind. The industrial capacity of workmen cannot be developed unless they live in reasonable comfort in houses in which they take a pride, provided with adequate sustenance and encouraged by the prospect of bettering their condition. It is not in countries where the standard of living is lowest, and the pleasures of hope are denied, that production is most rapid and economical. 'La pesanteur des charges,' said Montesquieu, ' produit d'abord le travail ; le travail l'accablement ; l'accablement l'esprit de paresse.'

I conclude with one practical suggestion. The labour problem will find its natural solution in an increased supply of labour. It is for this purpose that a handful of foreigners has been lately introduced. Would it not be more easy and more satisfactory to train up the youth of our own country in greater numbers to be skilled handicraftsmen ? The reluctance to perform manual labour is a great and growing evil—an evil which has its origin, not so much in a dislike to hard work, as in that false social system which gives to the man at the desk a higher rank than it accords to him who stands in a fustian jacket at the mason's bench. Popular education is good ; let us guard ourselves against its attendant risks. Let us take care that the educational advantages which we are now giving to the people are not perverted.

Mr. Plunkett quotes from the *Philadelphia Times* some very pertinent observations : ' What a terrible satire upon our boasted free school system is conveyed in the word " educated " ! Our children have their poor little brains crammed full of all kinds of impossible knowledge of names and dates and numbers, and unintelligible rules. There is absolutely no room left to hold any of the simple truths which former generations deemed more important than all the learning of the books. The result is, that they leave school ignorant of what is most essential, and outside of the schools there is no provision for their learning anything.'

It is by a courteous bearing in all the relations of life that the privileged classes can best testify their sense of the real dignity which attaches to honest labour, and show their conviction that the skilful labour of the hands is not inconsistent with culture and refinement.

DISCUSSION

Mr. G. E. Street, R.A., presided. The speakers included able representatives as well of the workmen as the employers. On the side of the workmen were Mr. George Howell and Mr. George Potter—names honoured and remembered by those who, in days gone by, carefully followed labour questions. Mr. Lucas and Mr. Trollope were able champions of the employers. The Chairman impartially summed up. He spoke with the commanding authority belonging to one who has designed some of the finest buildings of the present age : ' I have been very much pleased to see the good temper with which this discussion has been carried on, and my only regret is that we have not had more representatives of the masons and the working classes present than we have had. Unfortunately, I called upon one of them at the very outset, and put him in this way a little at a disadvantage, for which I have to apologise to him. I think that Mr. Brassey put before us very clearly the statement of the case—more clearly, indeed, than we have had it dealt with by anybody this evening. He pointed out very fairly that the in-creased cost of living, and of everything that the work-ing man has to provide, justified a considerable ad-vance of wages. The question, as he put it, appears to me to resolve itself into one simply of supply and demand. He has pointed out what has not been com-mented on to-night, and what is of the greatest im-portance, that the common labourer, who is not benefited by any trades society, has increased his wages during the period to the extent of about 64 per cent., while the skilled mechanic has only increased his by 50 per cent. Speaking for architects, but with the most kindly feeling for working men, I must say that the result of my experience is certainly very much to con-

firm what is said by Mr. Lucas and others on that side
—that we do not get at the present day the same amount
of work that we used to get, that the quality has not a
tendency to improve, and that, in spite of the statements which Mr. Howell and Mr. Potter make—that
they only fix the minimum amount any man may earn,
as a mere matter of fact, fixing a minimum rate must
almost always fix a uniform and maximum rate also.
The result is that we see, for instance, such a class as
the masons, with whom I personally am most concerned,
who work upon Gothic architecture—and it requires a
very skilled mason to make a good Gothic workman
—compelled to work—and it is monstrous that it should
be so—at the same wages as the man who does an
altogether inferior sort of work. Certainly on these
terms nobody will rise from a dead level. The workmen's object should be just what the object of the architect is, to encourage the good workman and to let the
rest see before them the example he sets, and the much
higher position in which he stands, by reason of his
ability and the superior quality, and perhaps quantity
too, of the work he does. How do you suppose men
rise in other professions ? By doing, not as little as
they can, but as much as they can, in hours far longer
than those of the workman, and therefore, if it is the
result of the action of trade societies that men are
limited in the amount of work they are allowed to do,
they are condemned, not by a hostile critic, but, in my
case, by one who is very anxious to see the working
man get his rights, and who is most emphatically opposed
to the notion of there being any " wickedness "—though
too often much want of prudence—in strikes. I see
no wickedness in a strike, so long as it is to obtain a
fair day's pay for a fair day's work. The wickedness
is when it prevents the best workman from earning
the best wages, and in spite of any denial one does often

find particular workmen objected to because they do too much work. I have myself known such cases as that quoted by Mr. Cates, and of which he gave us the particulars. They are not imaginary cases. An architect who goes about the country as I do meets with these difficulties in all directions, and knows that they do occur; and without knowing what all the rules are, and what all the exact decisions of the societies may be on the subject, that is one of the practical results of their action. The statement that they only insist upon a minimum amount of wages is at the same time met, unless I am very much mistaken, by the fact that, if a builder proposed to give two rates of wages, nearly all the men who work for him would probably absent themselves forthwith. My own experience is certainly of that kind. The societies undoubtedly interfere more or less with the freedom of the workman. The discussion we have had to-night, if it does nothing else, will show the representatives of the working classes how little hostility there is to them or to their true interest; and I must say that I think the speech of Mr. Lucas was creditable to him in every way. I trust that the outcome of all this will be that workmen will consider, if, at the present moment, they are defeated in the attempt they have made to raise their wages beyond a certain point, still that the masters have their interests necessarily just as much as their own in view; for what they have to consider is, whether in granting an increase of wages they will not be ruining the business that keeps them both? What Mr. Lucas has said about the replacement of brickwork by concrete is quite true. The tendency of the rules which the societies are making is to destroy all art. If we dare to have nothing but concrete done by labourers at the lowest wages, and if stone-masonry and good brickwork are to become things of the past, I think that good architecture will also entirely disappear from the field, and that we as architects shall have to give up our work. Therefore, in the interests of my profession, and in the interests of the workmen, I appeal to the representatives of the working men to-night to reconsider their position; and I do hope that sooner or later these rules of the societies (which are so mysterious that when they are quoted on the one side they are always denied on the other) shall be so far modified as to encourage good work and honest work, and to render it impossible for anybody long to say—as it has been said this evening, and in a way that most of us, from our experience, could confirm—that, as a rule, men do not feel it their duty to do the greatest amount of work in the best way and in the shortest time.'

CHAPTER IX

FOREIGN COMPETITION—COMPARATIVE EFFICIENCY
OF ENGLISH AND FOREIGN LABOUR

*(Reprinted from Volume on Foreign Work and
English Wages, published in 1879)*

BEFORE entering upon other subjects, some observations may not be superfluous with reference to the excess of our imports over our exports. It has been assumed that we have paid for our importations by calling in capital from abroad, and that the debts due to us from foreign nations have been rapidly diminishing in amount. A clear and satisfactory explanation of the disproportion in question has, however, been given by Mr. Shaw Lefevre in his address to the Statistical Society. Excess of imports over exports.

' The excess in the value of our imports over that of our exports has increased from the average of £58,000,000 in 1867–69 to £118,000,000 in 1875–77, and reached the enormous sum of £142,000,000 in 1877. Making, however, an addition of 10 per cent. to the value of our exports, in respect of freight, insurance and profit, and a deduction of 5 per cent. from the value of our imports in respect of freight and other charges, as Mr. Newmarch has explained is necessary, the difference is considerably reduced ; for the years 1863 to 1870 this difference averaged Mr. Shaw Lefevre's explanations.

£25,000,000 ; in 1871 it fell to £4,000,000 ; in 1872 there was an excess value of exports of £8,000,000 ; in 1873 the excess of imports was £12,000,000 ; in 1874, £26,000,000 ; in 1875, £47,000,000 ; in 1876, £77,000,000 ; in 1877, £97,000,000 ; and for ten months of the current year it is £74,000,000. Comparing the three years of great commercial activity, 1871–73, with the three last years, the total difference in value for the first period was £5,000,000, or nearly £2,000,000 a year, and for the last period £217,000,000 or £72,000,000 a year.'

Payments on capital invested abroad,

In this connection the remittances of dividends and interests on capital invested abroad must also be taken into view. Mr. Giffen has estimated the annual income from the capital so invested at £65,000,000. In the ten years, 1867–77, nearly £600,000,000 sterling must have been invested in foreign securities.

According to Mr. Seyd, the indebtedness of foreign countries to the United Kingdom is not less than from £1,000,000,000 to £1,100,000,000, bearing an annual interest of from £40,000,000 to £50,000,000. Making allowance for defaulters, the sum to be remitted annually to this country cannot be less than £30,000,000. In addition to these large remittances on private account, the Govern-

supplied by excess in value of imports.

ment draws some £15,000,000 a year on India. It is by the excess in the value of the imports that the vast sums annually due to England for interest on our foreign investments are paid, and the means provided for meeting the various charges, and for paying to us the profits we realise on our exported goods.

The large expenditure in England imposes a most serious burden on the finances in India. The revenue is singularly deficient in elasticity, and the mass of the people live from hand to mouth on mere subsistence wages. The interest on foreign loans, and the drawings on India, should be nearly sufficient to restore the balance between the value of the imports and the exports. But we must also bring into account the sums payable to this country in respect of the profits of trading on the goods exported and imported, and the earnings of the ships chiefly sailing under the British flag in which those goods are carried. The value at which imported goods are calculated includes every element of cost, freight, profit, commissions, and insurance. The value of the exports, on the other hand, is incomplete ; it is the mere cost of the manufacture, exclusive of freights, insurance, commissions and profits. Again, as M. Leroy Beaulieu points out, there is a natural tendency to undervalue goods exported to countries where heavy duties are levied *ad valorem*. Hence we find in the trade of every commercial or rather manufacturing nation, in a greater or less degree, a similar excess in the value of the imports over the exports.

The total importations of the commercial nations exceed their exportations by not less than 15 per cent. The table published in a statistical work by Dr. Neumann-Spellart gives the total importations and exportations for the five quarters of the globe.

Other counter-balancing facts.

—	Importations	Exportations
	Francs	Francs
Europe	28,202,000,000	21,681,000,000
America . . .	4,864,000,000	5,636,000,000
Asia	2,445,000,000	3,208,000,000
Australia . . .	1,189,000,000	1,122,000,000
Africa	672,000,000	783,000,000
Total . .	37,372,000,000	32,430,000,000

The nation not l¹ving beyond its means.

The causes of the disparity between the total values of the exports and imports have been explained in the preceding remarks, and it will be evident on a full consideration of the circumstances, that the apprehension that we are living as a nation beyond our means rests on no solid foundation. Indeed, as M. Leroy Beaulieu remarks, the magnitude of our import trade, so far from its affording a just ground for anxiety, must be´ regarded as a proof of the greatness of our resources and the stability of our power. The large balance against this country which formerly existed can be fully and satisfactorily explained, and a marked reduction in the excess value of our imports has recently taken place.

Alleged production of the crisis by foreign com- e on.

The crisis through which we are passing has been attributed by many to foreign competition. The true view was given by the Earl of Beaconsfield in the House of Lords. Our foreign competitors may have succeeded for a time in producing a limited number of articles at a lower cost or of a more convenient pattern, but we have not been beaten in any important branch of trade in a fair and open competition.

The articles imported in increased quantities are chiefly food and raw materials. For example, the goods sent to us by Russia, valued at £22,000,000 or £4,500,000 in excess of our importations in 1876, consisted mainly of corn, flax, linseed, sugar and tallow. The increased importations from Germany consisted of corn, potatoes and sugar. A certain increase was observable in the silk and woollen goods imported through Holland, but neither Belgium, France, nor Portugal showed any appreciable change in the value of the import trade from those countries. The import trade from the United States, amounting to the vast sum of £78,000,000, is composed almost exclusively of food and raw materials.

Nature of articles s imported

The main augmentation in the American exports in the interval from 1868 to 1878 consists of food and the raw materials of industry. The exportation of the principal manufactured articles is still on an insignificant scale.

Mr. Newmarch has shown in a clear and comprehensive tabular statement the conspicuous superiority of the United Kingdom over every other manufacturing country in respect to the exportation of articles of native production and manufacture. The subjoined table, with Mr. Newmarch's commentary on the figures, has been extracted from his able paper, recently read before the Statistical Society, on the progress of the Foreign Trade of the United Kingdom, 1856–77.

Our predominance in the export trade.

Imports (General) and Exports (Special or of Native Production and Manufacture), Four Periods, 1860–75. Totals per Head of Population. Five Leading Protectionist Countries.

Imports

Year	France (General)	Germany	Austria	Russia	United States	United Kingdom
	£	£	£	£	£	£
1860 .	125,000,000	—	32,000,000	25,000,000	74,000,000	210,000,000
1865 .	163,000,000	—	37,000,000	24,000,000	50,000,000	271,000,000
1869 .	160,000,000	—	60,000,000	54,000,000	87,000,000	295,000,000
1875 .	178,000,000	237,000,000	84,000,000	85,000,000	115,000,000	374,000,000
Increase	53,000,000	—	52,000,000	60,000,000	41,000,000	164,000,000

Imports per head

	France	Germany	Austria	Russia	United States	United Kingdom
	s.	s.	s.	s.	s.	s.
1860	68	—	20	7	48	140
1865	88	—	22	7	30	186
1869	88	—	34	14	46	196
1875	100	105	46	22	58	240
Increase	32	—	26	15	10	100

Exports

Year	France (General)	Germany	Austria	Russia	United States	United Kingdom
	£	£	£	£	£	£
1860 .	91,000,000	—	26,000,000	27,000,000	66,000,000	135,000,000
1865 .	123,000,000	—	34,000,000	32,000,000	28,000,000	165,000,000
1869 .	123,000,000	—	44,000,000	42,000,000	57,000,000	190,000,000
1875 .	155,000,000	176,000,000	50,000,000	60,000,000	104,000,000	225,000,000
Increase	64,000,000	—	24,000,000	33,000,000	38,000,000	90,000,000

Exports per head

	France	Germany	Austria	Russia	United States	United Kingdom
	s.	s.	s.	s.	s.	s.
1860	50	—	16	7	43	92
1865	66	—	20	8	18	115
1869	66	—	24	10	30	121
1875	84	80	28	16	54	142
Increase	34	—	12	9	11	52

Note.—As regards Germany, I find, on inquiry of Mr. Giffen, that there are as yet no official figures for 1860-65-69.

'It will scarcely be said that on the face of these figures the United Kingdom suffers in any particular when compared with any one of the four countries for which the imports and exports are given at each of the four dates during the sixteen years ; or indeed with all the four countries (France, Austria, Russia, and United States) in combination ; in other words, the 30,000,000 people in the United Kingdom, aided by Free Trade, bear most advantageous comparison with the 150,000,000 relying upon protection. Thus :

INCREASE IN IMPORTS, 1860–75.

Four foreign countries, France, Austria, Russia, and United States	£206,000,000 = 26s. per head.
United Kingdom	£164,000,000 = 100s. per head.

INCREASE IN EXPORTS, 1860–75.

Four foreign countries . . .	£160,000,000 = 22s. per head
United Kingdom	£90,000,000 = 52s. per head.

If the several countries be compared *singly* with the United Kingdom, as in fairness they should be, seeing that the population is about equal (Russia excepted), and the climate better, and the natural resources greater than the United Kingdom, not one of them exhibits progress in any degree approaching that of the United Kingdom.'

Mr. Newmarch proceeds to examine the statistics Unenumerated articles.

of the supplementary imports and exports—that is
to say, the large number of new and miscellaneous
articles which grow up year by year, and for the
sake of conciseness and uniformity, have to be
entered in the official tables under the title of
'Unenumerated Articles.' It will be found that
these two classes present the following highly
satisfactory results :

*Progress of Supplemental Imports and Exports.
United Kingdom, 1856–1877.   Declared Values.*

	1877	1870	1865	1860	1856
IMPORTS (a) Remainder of enumerated	£ 45,000,000	£ 17,000,000	£ 6,000,000	£ 4,000,000	£ 3,000,000
(b) Unenumerated . .	39,000,000	64,000,000	55,000,000	42,000,000	35,000,000
	84,000,000	81,000,000	61,000,000	46,000,000	38,000,000
Percentage of total Imports	Per cent. 21	Per cent. 25	Per cent. 22	Per cent. 21	Per cent. 22
EXPORTS (a) Remainder of enumerated	£ 21,000,000	£ 16,000,000	£ 10,000,000	£ 4,000,000	£ 5,000,000
(b) Unenumerated . .	17,000,000	11,000,000	8,000,000	9,000,000	8,000,000
	38,000,000	27,000,000	18,000,000	13,000,000	13,000,000
Percentage of total Exports	Per cent. 19	Per cent. 13	Per cent. 11	Per cent. 10	Per cent. 11

'We have here a doubling of the supplemental *imports* in the twenty-one years 1856–77, or from £38,000,000 to £84,000,000, the proportion of the total imports remaining at 21 per cent.

'The supplemental *exports* increase nearly three-fold, as from £13,000,000 to £37,000,000 and the proportion to the total exports rises from 11 to 19 per cent.'

The wise statesmanship which has generally distinguished the government of this country has placed our trade and commerce in the most favourable position for international competition. The 'Westminster Review,' in an article published on January 1, 1876, points out that in no other country but our own have wealth and population kept pace with debt.

The comparative lightness of the taxation is an obvious advantage in our favour. We possess advantages of climate to which Mr. Smith very properly adverted. Our climate may be fickle, and our skies obscured by clouds, but there is no season of year in which manual labour cannot be efficiently performed. Our working classes are free from the conscription which imposes such an oppressive burden on the populations of France and Germany. In the universal liability to military service the industry of those powers is burdened with a tax which more than neutralises any advantage they may possess in the comparative cheapness of labour. Mr. Smith summed up his able statement with a cheering and well-founded assertion that our working classes can, if they choose, beat all their

foreign rivals, both in the excellence and in the
thorough honesty and cheapness of their work,
and may thus maintain their long-established
supremacy in the markets of the world.

Beneficial
results of
free trade
in
England.
In his paper on the Progress of the Foreign
Trade with the United Kingdom, from which we
have already quoted, Mr. Newmarch has given
an exhaustive enumeration of the beneficial results
of the bold and enlightened fiscal policy adopted
in our own country. He appropriately refers to the
inauguration of free trade by Sir Robert Peel in
1846, and to the advice tendered by that great
statesman, that the best way to compete with
hostile tariffs was to encourage free imports. At
the end of a generation, as Mr. Newmarch points
out, having faithfully followed Sir Robert Peel's
advice, we have seen our imports rise from
£70,000,000 to £380,000,000, and a fabulous accumulation of wealth has been formed in the
country. By our free trade system the United
Kingdom has become the great mart of the world
for the exchange of merchandise, and for settling
international claims. It has given rise to what
Mr. Newmarch designates as a triangular system
of trade which goes very far to neutralise the evils
of protective tariffs.

'The United States cannot help taking tea and
silk from China, and cannot help China refusing to
take tobacco and raw cotton in exchange. Hence
the United States cannot help sending the tobacco
and raw cotton to England, and using the proceeds
in the purchase of English credits available to

discharge the China debt. In like manner it is every day more true that England pays for a large part of its imports not directly to the country A from whence they come, but indirectly to other countries to which A happens to be in debt.

'The true nature of foreign trade is that the nations of the world should resemble not merely a single country, but a large town within that country, throughout the streets, lanes and alleys of which there shall be kept up as constant, rapid and easy a current of dealings as prevails among the natives of the town itself.'

Mr. Newmarch steadfastly maintains that tried by every statistical test, the extraordinary growth of our foreign trade and the accumulation of capital in the United Kingdom have been the result of steady adherence to the free trade maxims of

(1) Cultivating the imports, and leaving the exports to cultivate themselves ;

(2) Regarding the benefit of the consumer as the paramount object to be attained.

While experience has shown that free trade has conferred immense benefits on Great Britain, it cannot be doubted that it would have been a still better thing if the same enlightened principles had been more universally adopted.

It is not from the cheap labour of Belgium, as the writers of the manifestoes from time to time issued by the associations of employers would have us believe, but from the dear but skilful and energetic labour of the United States, that the most formidable competition will hereafter arise. Mr. Gladstone,

Future commercial supremacy of America.

in his contribution to the *North American Review*, entitled ' Kin beyond Sea,' has rightly said that the commercial supremacy of the world must ultimately pass from the United Kingdom to the United States. The territory at their command is, in comparison with the narrow area of the United Kingdom, unlimited, and it possesses every natural advantage. The soil is fertile ; the mineral wealth is inexhaustible ; and the increase in the population has been so rapid that Professor Huxley has predicted that when the second centenary of the republic is celebrated, the American people will have increased from 40,000,000 to 200,000,000.

Sir J. Hawk-shaw's testimony to the progress of her people.
The marvellous energy of this vast population in utilising the great resources of their country called forth the approving testimony of Sir John Hawk-shaw in his report on the Exhibition at Philadelphia : ' The 70,000 miles of railway already constructed, the ramifications of the electric telegraph, and its application to uses more extended and varied even than in our own country, the crowd of steamboats wherever navigation is possible and public convenience can be promoted, the building of cities like Chicago, which after the great fire in four or five years has arisen out of its ashes a more beautiful city than before—all these tell of the increase of wealth, and speak still more strongly of the public and patriotic spirit of the people.

' To me who visited the United States on a former occasion, but so long ago that Chicago was then but a village, and Philadelphia had not more than one half its present population, when its railways were only beginning to be made, with wooden bridges and temporary works, when its vast mineral wealth was nearly untouched, and wood was burned where coal is now consumed, the astonishing changes, and the vast progress since made, appear greater than perhaps to others whose visits have been more frequent.'

That the United States must hereafter command a dominant position is certain, but there is no immediate prospect of a competition which can be injurious to our own manufacturers.   The American export trade is continually increasing, both in bulk and value, but hitherto the growth in the export of manufactured goods has been unimportant.   Agricultural products constitute the great bulk of their export trade.   The success of the American manufacturers, in so far as it depends on the effective application of labour, is certainly not due to the low scale of wages.   On the contrary it is the high price of labour which has been the main incentive to the application of the national genius to the invention of labour-saving machinery.

The surprising economic results which followed American the outbreak of the Civil War are thus described labour-saving by Mr. Wells : ' The outbreak of Civil War in 1861, machi-and its vigorous prosecution until 1865, acted as an nery. immense stimulus to invention and discovery in the Northern States, and led to an application of labour-saving machinery and methods to the work of production which, taking time into consideration, has probably no parallel in the world's experience. . . . . With certainly not more than five millions of male adults engaged in agriculture, mechanic arts, manufactures, and transportation in the Northern States in 1860, the close of the war, in 1865, found more than a million of adults enrolled in the service of the Northern armies.   But the industrial products of these same States, especially the products of agriculture, did not in general decrease during the war period by reason of the diversion of labour noted, but on the contrary, and mainly through the invention and use of labour-saving machinery, they largely increased.   Thus, for example, the amount of wheat raised in Indiana in 1859 was 15,219,000 bushels, but in 1863, notwithstanding that this State, out of a population in 1860 of 1,350,000, had furnished to the army more than 124,000 fighting men, its product of wheat exceeded 20,000,000 bushels ;   and what was true of Indiana was also true of Iowa, Illinois, and other agricultural States, and in respect to productions other than wheat.'

By ingenious mechanical labour the Americans are now competing successfully against the cheap manual labour of Switzerland, and we learn from the report of Mr. Beauclerk, the Secretary of the Legation at Berne, for the year 1878, that the diminished exportation of watches to the United States has inflicted severe losses on the hand-workers in Switzerland.

Farming in the Western States.

Industry and ingenuity have enabled the Americans to conquer in a remarkable degree the many difficulties which obstruct their industrial development ; but while a wide extent of soil remains untilled, the most profitable and congenial occupation of the people must be pastoral and agricultural rather than manufacturing.

The natural expansion of the population over the plains of the West was for a time arrested by the high protective duties which secured excessive profits to manufacturers, and led to a development of production beyond the requirements of the country. A reaction has naturally followed from the excessive development of manufacturing industry. Of 716 furnaces in existence in 1877, 446 are out of blast, and the workmen are rapidly leaving the factories and ironworks and resorting to the unsettled lands in the Western States. The rapid growth of Kansas may be taken as an example of the impetus given to an agricultural State by the extensive migration from the manufacturing districts. The population has increased since 1875 from 531,000 to 700,000. In 1872 the entire number of acres under cultivation in the State was 2,476,862, and the value of the product thereof 25,265,109 dollars. In 1877 the acres under cultivation reached 5,595,304, and the value of the product therefrom 45,597,051 dollars. In 1878 the acres under cultivation exceeded 6,500,000, the increase being nearly a million acres in a single year. A similar movement, though of course on a smaller scale, is taking place in our own country, where agricultural labour is gradually returning from the furnaces to the farms. *Growth o Kansas.*

The migration from the industrial centres to the agricultural States of the West is prominently noticed in the annual report of the American *Migration of artisans:*

mercantile agency of Messrs. Dun & Co., quoted by the 'Economist' in the annual review of the trade of 1878. The sales of land by the national government increased from 3,338,000 acres in the year ending the 30th of June, 1877, to 7,562,000 acres in the succeeding year. An equal increase has taken place in the sale of lands by the State land agencies and railroad land offices. It is estimated that no less than 20,000,000 acres were newly settled in 1878, and that not less than 100,000 families, representing a population of half a million, have changed their abodes and their pursuits in the same period.

ts
nfluence
m wages.

Wages can never long remain at a low level in the United States, while the working man can transport himself and his family from the irksome employment of the factory to the free life of the Western plains. The profits realised upon agriculture in the Mississippi Valley, as the 'Economist' observes, exercise a paramount influence in determining the average rate of wages in the manufacturing industries of the United States. The prospects of agriculture in the West were never more favourable than at the present time, and we have, therefore, reason to believe that the cost of industrial labour will be sustained for some time to come on the existing scale. As an evidence of the attractions of an agricultural life to populations engaged in factories and ironworks, I may refer to the fact mentioned by Mr. Henderson in his recent paper in the 'Contemporary Review,' that on the average the working staff of the American factories is changed once in three years.

In a paper contributed to the 'Fortnightly Mutation Review' by Mr. Atkinson, of Boston, we are informed of the factory that during the last thirty years the factory popula- popula- tion of New England has passed through three tion. phases. First came the sons and daughters of the New England farmer; but they have now betaken themselves to easier and better paid employments. The native operatives of New England were succeeded by the Irish; but the Irish, in their turn, saved money, and bought the farms deserted by the New England yeomen who had emigrated to the richer lands in the west. French Canadians now supply the labour formerly furnished by the Irish emigration, and, it is said, exhibit in manufacturing industry a vigour and energy of which they gave no indications while dwelling on their little strips of land on the banks of the River St. Lawrence. It will be admitted that American industrial enterprise has made great progress, and that an abundant supply of labour will at all times be furnished by emigration; but for the reasons which have been enumerated, commodities in the production of which labour is a principal factor, must at the present time be cheaper in England than in the United States, although our goods may be excluded from the American market by a prohibitory tariff.

M

Comparative Efficiency of English and Foreign Labour.

Wages not answerable for collapses of trade. I now proceed to discuss the character and conduct of the British workman, always so severely criticised in a time of commercial depression. When trade expands and every available man finds employment, wages inevitably rise. When trade collapses it is said, and often most unjustly, that the inflation of wages has been the main cause of our disasters. It is owing to the constant and unnecessary augmentation of our manufacturing resources that the market has been overstocked, and that a general depreciation of prices has been brought about.

Our loss of trade apparent with protected countries, If we test the comparative efficiency of British labour by the amount of our exports, we shall see that we have lost ground chiefly in our trade with the great manufacturing countries where the supply of capital and labour has been abundant, and where we have to encounter a serious protective tariff. It is in those very countries in which the growth of manufactures has been most rapid, and against which we have been told to be on our guard as formidable rivals, that the apprehension of British competition is most keenly felt. The progress of our trade with non-manufacturing countries and in neutral markets is not unsatisfactory.

not in neutral markets. The following figures are taken from the Board of Trade tables. The comparison is made between

1873, when our exports were at the highest point they have ever attained, and 1877 :

Countries	Exports	
	1873	1877
Java and other possessions in the Indian Seas . . .	£ 774,673	£ 2,088,775
Algeria	65,565	276,000
The Philippines	439,177	1,314,169
Morocco	365,364	465,258
Venezuela	541,620	633,740
Ecuador	109,383	255,618
Japan	1,884,145	2,460,275
British possessions . . .	71,147,707	75,752,150

It is difficult to obtain an impartial opinion on the subject of our investigation from persons practically familiar with the capabilities of the working man. In pursuing my inquiry I have keenly felt the loss of the valuable counsels of my late father. He had enjoyed unequalled opportunities of comparing the industrial powers of many nations. He felt generously towards the working man, and he was ever ready to pay liberally for vigorous and efficient labour.

In seeking for opinions on this difficult question of the relative efficiency of English and foreign labour, it is before all things necessary that the witnesses should be free from bias. I would rather take the opinion of a literary man or of an economist than that of a manufacturer on such a subject.

English compared with foreign labour.

M 2

Defoe's compari-son of English and Dutch labourers. Mr. Lecky, in his 'History of the Eighteenth Century,' quotes a passage from Defoe's pamphlet entitled 'Giving Alms no Charity,' which gives a vivid picture of the labouring men of England in the beginning of the last century. A bad system of poor relief had already wrought a pernicious influence on the peasantry. 'I affirm,' says Defoe, in the passage quoted by Mr. Lecky, 'of my own know-ledge that when I wanted a man for labouring work, and offered 9*s.* per week to strolling fellows at my door, they have frequently told me to my face that they could get more a begging. Good husbandry is no English virtue. . . .. . It neither loves nor is beloved by an Englishman. The English get fortunes, and the Dutch save them ; and this observation I have made between Dutchmen and Englishmen, that where an Englishman earns his 20*s.* a week and but just lives, as we call it, a Dutch-man with the same earnings grows rich, and leaves his children in a very good condition. Where an English labouring man with his 9*s.* a week lives wretchedly, a Dutchman with the same money will live tolerably.'

Dutch labourers at the present time. By the kindness of Mr. Watson who has had extensive experience in the construction of public works in Holland, I am enabled to give some facts which show how the Englishman compares with the Dutchman in our own day, nearly two centuries after Defoe's pamphlet was written.

In summer the Dutch mechanic begins his day's labour at 5 a.m. and ends at 7 p.m., with $2\frac{1}{2}$ hours' interval. In winter he commences work at 7 a.m. and ends at 5.30 p.m., with pauses of an hour and

a half. The workman's food costs from 1s. 3d. to
1s. 6d. a day. The English labourer, who consumes
more meat and beer, would probably spend from
2s. to 2s. 6d.

Education amongst Dutch mechanics is more
advanced than with us. Carpenters and bricklayers can generally understand and work to a
drawing, and write and read fluently.

With the view of comparing the cost of work in
Holland and in England, Mr. Watson analysed the
cost of some sea locks executed in Holland in 1870,
1871 and 1872. The brickwork cost £1 1s. 2d. per
cubic yard. On a railway contract near London,
executed in 1878, the price of ordinary brickwork
was found to be £1 4s. 4d. per yard. The quality
of the Dutch work is better than the English.
The bricks are excellent, and the workmanship
cannot be surpassed. In Holland the wages of a
good bricklayer average 3s. 10d. per day of ten hours.
The Englishman will do about the same amount of
work, but his wages for ten hours of labour in or
near London, until a recent date, were about 8s.
a day.

Extending the comparison to earth work, the
cubic yard costs by Dutch labour 3.02d.; by
English labour 3.63d. The transport of earth to
long distances is of rare occurrence in Holland. In
this particular the men are not expert, and the work
is quite as costly as in England.

Carpenters for rough work are paid in Holland
from 4d. to 4¾d. per hour. They are good workmen,
but not so active as Englishmen. It may be assumed
that the labour of four Englishmen would be equal

to that of five Dutchmen ; but the four Englishmen, at the London price of 6s. 6d. per day, would cost £1 6s. as compared with the sum of 18s. 9d. which would be paid for the five Dutchmen—thus making the English work about 46 per cent. dearer than the Dutch. The quality of the carpenters' work is excellent, but joiners cannot compete in quality or finish with London workmen.

In a report made by the director of a large engineering establishment at Amsterdam to the proprietors, comparing the Thames and the Clyde prices and results with those obtained on his own works, it is assumed that three Englishmen would accomplish as much as four Dutchmen, but the wages of the former averaged 8d. per hour, and the wages of the latter were 5d. As regards quality, though not equal in finish to London work, excellent steam-engines and machinery are now turned out of the Dutch establishments.

The cost of labour of all descriptions in Holland has risen at least 30 per cent. during the last ten years, with a corresponding rise in the cost of living.

It will be observed that Mr. Watson sets the cost of labour in the rural districts of Holland in comparison with its cost in the vicinity of London during a period of exceptional activity in the building trades. I cannot, therefore, accept his statement as a final judgment. We should take the prices paid for piece-work in the provinces, and the rates of wages paid throughout a period of at least ten years, in order to arrive at a fair average.

Gangs of navvies are to be seen at work at the present day in the vicinity of London, composed of men whose physical power and energy have never been exceeded in any former generation. They are worthy successors of the stalwart delvers of the earth who excavated the canals and constructed our vast network of railways. Having witnessed with the highest admiration the performances of the Lincolnshire labourers recently employed upon the extension of the Victoria Docks, I addressed some inquiries to Messrs. Lucas & Aird as to the amount of work executed and the remuneration paid to the navvies. It should be explained that the depth of the excavation is about thirty feet below the level upon which the excavated earth is deposited. The earth to be removed consisted mostly of heavy clay and peat. It is cut up with a grafting tool into cubes twelve inches deep by ten inches by nine inches, and carefully packed on the barrows, which will hold about ten pieces. Each barrow-load weighs from $3\frac{1}{2}$ to 4 hundredweight. Four navvies are employed in filling the barrows and running them to the foot of an incline. The runner runs his barrow with the assistance of a horse up the incline, making an ascent of thirty feet in perpendicnlar height, at an angle of perhaps sixty degrees. Having arrived at the summit of the incline, he wheels the barrow a distance of eighteen yards to the tip. The average quantity these men fill in one day is about eighteen cubic yards of clay and twenty-two cubic yards of peat. Their average earnings are 7s., and they work about eight hours per day.

The quantity of victuals they consume may be estimated at 2 lbs. of meat, 2 lbs. of bread, but not so much vegetables in proportion. Ale is their principal drink, of which they consume about five quarts during the working hours. On Monday morning these men are remarkable for a great display of clean white clothes in which they begin their week's work. As a rule they are quiet, and with a few exceptions are civil to those in charge of the work, and so long as they are fairly treated give little trouble.

The average stature of the Lincolnshire navvies is not inferior to the standard of the Household Cavalry, and the development of physical strength in their sinewy frames is greater in proportion as their labours are more arduous than those of a mounted trooper in the piping times of peace.

It would have been interesting to examine the cost of engineering works in all parts of Europe, and materials are not wanting ; time and space, however, do not admit of such an investigation on the present occasion. We will therefore proceed

Cost of labour at ironworks and collieries in France.

to examine the comparative cost of labour in the mines and iron works. Mr. Lowthian Bell is a high authority on this subject. With reference to the cost of labour in the ironworks and collieries in France, the inquiries instituted by Mr. Lowthian Bell in 1867 furnish ample information. Comparing the wages paid in France with the British standard, Mr. Lowthian Bell reported that blast-furnace keepers in France were satisfied with 4s. for a day's wages, a low rate no doubt as compared with English wages, but every French furnace had a second keeper. Mr. Lowthian Bell took infinite pains to obtain correct data as to the quality of the work and the quantity of iron made at each furnace. He found that at the furnaces on the Tees twenty-five individuals performed an amount of work identical with that executed by forty-two men at a French furnace. In spite, therefore, of the wages being, as nearly as he could estimate, 20 per cent. cheaper, the cost of the labour employed in smelting a ton of pig-iron was sensibly greater at the French works than at Middlesbrough.

The enhanced value of provisions had produced the same influence on the price of labour in Belgium as in France. Colliers worked in six-hour shifts and went down the pit twice in the twenty-four hours ; they worked, therefore, twelve hours a day, and earned from 2s. to 2s. 4¾d. per shift. A blast-furnace keeper only earned 2s. 4¾d. to 2s. 9½d. per day ; but then he had such help as brought up the cost of this description of labour to 6½d. to 7d. a ton for foundry iron, and for forge iron to a trifle above 4d. There were two chargers to each furnace, who, however, only received 2s. a day. The women were chiefly employed in coke burning and their wages were 1s. a day. In Belgium the same want of appliances for the saving of labour at the furnaces was observed as in France ; the result being that, notwithstanding the low rate of wages, the sum paid on a ton of iron in Belgium was about the same as in England.

The following comparative data are taken from a

In Belgium

in the United States.

paper written on the occasion of **Mr. Lowthian Bell's** visit to the Exhibition at Philadelphia :

Coal-hewers	'Hours of actual Work	Tons of Coal daily	Daily Net Earnings
			s. *d.*
Durham	5·39	3·90	5 0
Northumberland . . .	5·52	3·15	4 9
United States (bituminous coal)	10·0	5·00	8 6

The average earnings throughout Great Britain were about 5s. 2d. per day, or 11¼d. per hour of actual work. In 1874 the rates were 1s. 2d. per hour, for which the quantity worked was about 11 cwt. per man. In Northumberland and Durham the miners are supplied with firing and live rent-free, which makes their wages worth an additional 1½d. per hour, as compared with the earnings of colliers in the United States.

In America in 1874 the hewers got 13 cwt. of coal and were paid about 1s. 1d. per hour. It thus appears that at that date the advantage was rather on the side of the pitmen of this country.

In November 1874 the price paid for puddling iron on the Tees was 10s. 9d. per ton ; the average price in the United States at the same date was £1 0s. 7d. Since 1874 the price at Middlesbrough, has been reduced from 10s. 9d. to 8s. 3d., or 2s. 6d. per ton. During the same period the amount of reduction in the United States varied from 2s. to 4s. 6d. per ton ; but these concessions had been obtained at the expense of considerable interruptions to work and some serious disturbances.

Mr. Lowthian Bell could detect no difference between the Old and the New Country in the skill of manipulation exhibited by the workmen employed in the rolling-mills. The cost for labour per ton was fully 25 per cent. higher in America than in our own country.

Mr. Lowthian Bell gives the following as the earnings of workmen employed in ironworks on the continent of Europe for the year 1873, the period of the highest wages in this country and in America :

	Coal-hewers	Ironstone Miners	Puddlers (12 hours)		
		s. d. s. d.		*s. d. s. d.*	
Belgium	4*s.* to 7*s.* 2*d.* in 8 hours	2 6 to 3 7 per day	1st hand, 5 6 2nd „ 2 10 to 3 2		
Silesia .	3*s.* 6*d.* in 10 hours	1 10 in 8 hours	1st „ 4 9 2nd „ 3 2		

It is satisfactory to know that, after his wide and searching inquiry both in the United Kingdom and in America, Mr. Lowthian Bell arrives at the conclusion that in regard to cheapness and efficiency of the labour the workmen engaged in the ironworks of Great Britain have nothing to fear from foreign competition, even where the hours are longer and the scale of wages measured by the day is much lower than in our own country.

We shall now proceed to give some information bearing on the comparative efficiency of workmen employed in mining.

The comparison i favour of England.

Mr. Lumley, in his report on the Belgian coal trade for 1876, gives details as to the average output of coal per man in the province of Hainault :

Years	1st Division	2nd Division	3rd Division	Average for whole Province
	Tons	Tons	Tons	Tons
1867	157	193	198	180
1868	151	209	204	183
1869	156	215	217	190
1870	162	211	215	191
1871	158	212	206	188
1872	178	224	229	206
1873	169	202	210	191
1874	152	184	193	174
1875	157	191	195	178
1876	155	192	184	174
Average	159	203	205	185

From this table it appears that the productive power of the workman has not increased, the fact being that it does not depend solely on the progress of the industry, but also on the will and the calculations of the workman, who regulates his production according to his impressions of the position of the trade and the future course of prices.

The average wages in the Hainault collieries in 1876 were £41 8s. per man, a reduction of £5 15s. on the previous year. When business is brisk, the Belgian miner is not afraid to work his best, ' knowing that his wages will not be questioned ; when demand wanes and he sees no chance of a revival, he diminishes his production for fear of having his wages reduced. This accounts for the increase of 1866 and the subsequent fall, and for the improve-

ment which took place during the revival towards
the end of 1869 and the beginning of 1870, but
which was succeeded by a decrease during 1870 and
1871.'

It is somewhat curious to observe how dia-
metrically different is the conduct of the Belgian
and the English miner under the same conditions.
Let us compare the Belgian figures with some
English statistics, extracted from the columns of
the *Times*.

Superior
pro-
ductive
capacity
of the
British
miner.

In 1861 the industrial census shewed that 385,000
miners were employed to get 86,000,000 tons of coal,
showing an average of 223.3 tons of coal raised per
man. Last year, however, 494,000 miners raised
134,610,000 tons of coal, being an average of 272.4
tons per man.

The last reports of the Inspectors of Mines give
the output of minerals in the collieries of the United
Kingdom. Mr. Dickenson gives the average in the
districts of North and East Lancashire at 301 tons
per person employed, being an increase of 23 tons
per head. He attributes the increase to the efforts
of the miner to make up for lower wages. From the
mining districts of Scotland Mr. Alexander gives
the output per workman for 1873 at 256 tons,
increasing in 1877 to 318 tons. Mr. Evans reports
as follows from the Midland district : ' The quantity
of minerals raised during the year was 13,000,000
tons, giving employment to 50,285 persons. In the
year immediately preceding this the production was
about 12,500,000 tons, persons employed 52,448.
This shows that a decrease of 2163 persons worked
half a million more tons of coal than the year before.'

The relative capacity of the miners in Belgium and England may be measured by the difference between the output in the province of Hainault and the general average for the United Kingdom. In the one case it is 272 tons per man, in the other 185 tons. I believe the average relative industrial capability of the workmen of the two countries approximates very closely to the proportion which the output from the English miners bears to the output from the Belgian.

Energy of the British operative.

The Manchester correspondent of the *Times* gives the following illustration of the endurance of our operatives and of their energy and capacity for making a rational use of adversity.

' In a large mill where the wages paid before the late reduction were £500 a week, and where the simple reduction of 10 per cent. would leave the amount £450, it turned out that after the reduction had been submitted to, the employers had £510 to pay instead of any smaller sum. The explanation is that the workpeople had been more diligent at their looms, and by this effort of self-discipline some of them, if not all, earned more money at the reduced rate than they had earned before the strike. They also did more work, and produced a larger quantity of cloth at the cheaper rate, so that their employers could afford to sell it more cheaply in proportion ; and they contributed in their degree towards swelling the production which their leaders are so anxious to limit. They were not to be blamed, but commended, for making the best of their own situation.'

The industrial capabilities of Germany are seriously impaired by the disaffection of the workmen to the Government and the established order of things, both social and commercial. A well-informed contributor to the 'Edinburgh Review' of July 1878 states that German workmen abhor all forms of religion as antagonistic to socialism. The great commercial centres afford a congenial soil for the new doctrines.

In the debates in 1876 on the German Criminal Supplementary Law, Prince Bismarck declared that the Socialist Press 'contributed to cause the stagnation of trade, and to make a German working day less productive than a French or English working day.' The Prince referred the members of the Reichstag in proof of this to their own observation of Frenchmen working by the side of Germans in Berlin ; and he declared anyone could see that a French builder executed in a day more and better work than a German ; the result is that German work cannot compete in the world's markets with French. Prince Bismarck traced the decline to Socialist agitation for undefined and unrealisable objects, and he was not sanguine of any cure for the disease except poverty.' Commenting on Prince Bismarck's observations, the 'Edinburgh Reviewer' very truly observes that poverty is the most certain cure for the onslaught which labour designs against capital. If the Socialist schemes were carried into effect, the workmen would speedily find that capital does something more than feed on their earnings. The practical consequences of social disaffection in

German labour and Socialism.

Germany were brought out at a conference of the several shipowning associations of Germany recently held at Berlin. It was stated that German shipowners had been compelled to have recourse to foreign shipbuilding yards, their own workmen being unsteady and unreliable, and entirely under the pernicious influence of trades unions and socialistic associations.

Inferiority of German to British workmen.

An interesting comparison of the relative capabilities of English and German workmen was lately given in the 'Leeds Mercury,' from an occasional correspondent, the result of inquiries made in Prussia, in Saxony, in Bohemia, in Austria, in Hungary, and in Roumania.

' " We find our Englishmen," said one gentleman who employs about a score of English mechanics along with three or four score North Germans, " by far the best men we can possibly get. I have no doubt, indeed, that a single Englishman is worth two Germans."

' " In what way ? " I asked.

' " In the power of using his head as well as his hands. Your German mechanic can do his routine work very well, and he will do it at wages of only half the amount paid to an Englishman, but let him get into any difficulty—such as the breakdown of part of the machinery—and you see at once his inferiority to his English colleague. He doesn't know what to do, but his first idea is that he must make a great noise, and let everybody know that a terrible misfortune has happened. Then if by any accident he is able to put the thing right again, he gets all the more credit from his master for his wonderful achievement ; whilst if, on the other hand, he cannot do anything, he has the satisfaction of knowing that nobody has expected him to succeed in repairing the mischief. The Englishman, however, in such a case says nothing to anybody, but he looks about him, finds out for himself where the injuries are, uses his wits, and gets the thing put right again before anybody is aware that an accident has happened."

' " Yes," interrupted one of my companions who happened to have a special knowledge of the subject, " but remember that you are speaking of picked Englishmen, carefully selected for you out of one of the largest manufacturing shops in Great Britain. You will not find that the average English workman has anything like the superiority to the average German that you claim for him."

' " I am not so sure of that," pursued my original informant. " It is true that mine are picked men, but I have the pick of the Germans also, and my conclusion is that whilst the German may be trusted to do a routine piece of work, in which he has been thoroughly trained, nearly, if not quite, as well as the Englishman, in all labour in which you use your head, or, as Opie said, ' mix your colours with brains,' the Englishman ranks far before all foreigners." '

Very recently it has been determined to man the engine-rooms and stoke-holes of the French mail

N

steamers running between Dover and Calais with Frenchmen. It is a significant circumstance that one Englishman is still to be retained as second engineer. In case a bad breakdown should occur, it is needless to say that the entire responsibility would devolve on our fellow-countryman.

The textile industries: Mr. Mundella's comparison of British and foreign labour.

Turning to the textile industries we have in Mr. Mundella a most competent authority, from personal experience both in Nottingham and on the Continent. He tells us that the Englishman, though much less sober, less instructed, and less refined, is yet more inventive, and can give more good suggestions to his master than the artisan of any other country.

Mr. Mundella has published a valuable collection of evidence in a paper on the 'Conditions on which the Commercial and Manufacturing Supremacy of Great Britain depends,' which was read before the Statistical Society in March 1878. He says that 'no question has been so fully discussed as that of the present efficiency of English labour. According to some, both its quality and productiveness have declined in proportion as its costliness has increased. While expressing my belief that much that has been said has been unnecessarily severe and in some instances grossly unjust, it is impossible to deny that the high wages earned in the coal and iron trades during the late period of inflation have added little to the material or moral well-being of many of the workers in these branches of industry. But if this is true, as I fear it is of too many, it is not true of all.* A sudden and exceptional rise of the rate of profits or of wages in any branch of business is seldom more than temporary, and rarely brings with it lasting benefit to either employer or employed. This part of our inquiry has such an important bearing upon the question under consideration, that I propose to consider it more fully than any other. . . .

'While fully and painfully conscious of the defects of my countrymen, and regretful as any man of that recklessness, intemperance, and thriftlessness which are the characteristics of too many, and which have led them to waste the opportunities afforded them by a time of exceptional prosperity, I am of opinion that their energy, efficiency and skill have suffered no diminution, and that they are to-day, as they have been in the past, superior in these qualities to the workmen of any other nation. There is a strenuousness of effort, a rapidity and deftness in their movements which I have never seen equalled except in the United States. The American, being of the same race, I rank as the equal of the Englishman. I do not believe he is superior, only so far

* Mr. J. W. Pease, M.P., in giving evidence before the Coal Committee of 1873, said : ' I found from the secretary of one of the building societies, that he had on his books 268 pitmen from the district in which our collieries are worked. . . . Those men had deposited in the year 1872, £3900. Another secretary said that from looking over his books he found that the men in the group of collieries just named had deposited, on an average, £300 a month in his building society.'

as he excels in temperance and intelligence. This opinion is founded upon long experience, personal observation, and the evidence afforded by competent and impartial witnesses. I have often in my **own** experience compared the production of French, German and American workmen with that of the English, from machinery in every case made in England, and I have never known the Frenchman or German to produce the same quantity of work as the Englishman, although their working hours were longer. Generally the production fell short from 20 to 25 per cent. The American under equal conditions will produce nearly, though not quite, as much. Wherever I have found him producing more, it was due to his having been furnished with better machinery and appliances to work with. Where considerable physical strength is required in connection with technical skill, I have invariably found the continental workman much slower than the Englishman, and the production in this case not more than two-thirds of our own. It is quite true that even more than a corresponding reduction is made from the wages, but this does not compensate for the diminished productiveness of the capital, machinery and plant employed, and for the consequent increase in the working expenses.

' In a lecture delivered by Mr. Alexander Redgrave, in November 1871, before the Philosophic Institute of Bradford, he gives the following statistics as to the proportion of spindles to persons employed in the cotton factories of the various continental States :

In France	. . . 14	In Belgium	. . . 50
„ Russia	. . . 28	„ Saxony	. . . 50
„ Prussia	. . . 37	„ Switzerland	. . 55
„ Bavaria	. . . 46	„ Smaller States of	
„ Austria	. . . 49	Germany	. . 55
		„ United Kingdom	. 74

' " Incidentally," he adds, " the following statements have been made to me by managers of cotton factories, showing the relative capacity of work of the Englishman and foreigner.

' " In Germany the working hours were (at that time) from 5.30 a.m. to 8.30 p.m. every day, including Saturday. In a cotton factory there a manager calculated that the same weight was produced when superintended by English over-lookers as in sixty hours in England ; but if the work was superintended by German overlookers, the weight produced would be much less.

' " As another instance : In Russia the factories work night and day one hundred and fifty hours per week, there being two sets each working seventy-five hours per week. Taking the year round, the manager of a cotton factory there considered that, in England, as much would be produced in sixty hours per week. He also said that no weaver ever had more than two looms, and that the speed of the machinery was about one-third less than in this country." '

Some few years since I had opportunities of inquiring into this subject, both in France and in

Germany, and from every quarter, and especially from English overlookers, I received the strongest assurances that the English workman was un-approachable in the amount of good work turned out and in steadiness, that the relative cheapness of wages did not counterbalance the steadiness and quickness of the Englishman at his work.

I have reason to know that the proportion of spindles to operatives employed on the Continent, quoted by Mr. Redgrave in 1871, has in the interim considerably augmented. Improved machinery has in the same period been largely introduced in our own cotton-mills, while the hours of continental labour have considerably diminished, and the wages increased. The restrictions on the employment of children and young persons are now more severe in France, Germany and Switzerland than with us.

From M. Taine's well-known 'Notes on England' we draw the following comparison between the English and French workman.

After referring to the more salient types of British workmen, to their strongly nourished, hardy and active frames, their phlegmatic, cool, and perse-vering natures, he thus continues :

'French manufacturers tell me that with them the workman labours perfectly during the first hour, less efficiently during the second, still less during the third, and so goes on diminishing in efficiency, until in the last hour he does little good at all. His muscular force flags, and above all, his attention becomes relaxed. Here [in England], on the con-trary, the workman labours as well during the last

as the first hour ; but, on the other hand, his work-
day is one of ten hours and not of twelve, as with
us.   By reason, however, of this better sustained
attention, the Englishman gets through more work.
At Messrs. Shaw's, of Manchester, to manage 2400
spindles one man and two children are found
sufficient ; in France it needs two men and three,
four, and sometimes more children for the same
purpose. . . . . . But in certain qualities ' (says
M. Taine), ' as in the matter of taste, artistic finish,
and the like, the Frenchman has the advantage.
He is more *imaginative*, less mechanical, and by consequence that power of concentration, of stubborn,
persevering and sustained application where the
labour is monotonous, which so distinguishes the
English workman and gives him his pre-eminence,
is lacking in the French.'

In 1873 a circular was addressed to Her Majesty's
representatives abroad at the instance of the National
Association of Factory Occupiers, requesting them to
furnish information as to the spinning and weaving
of textile fabrics in the countries to which they were
accredited.   This was in anticipation of the factory
legislation which took place in the following year.
In Belgium, where there are no legislative restrictions, and where labour is cheap and abundant,
Mr. Kennedy, our representative, reported ' that
the flax and cotton industries have remained
stationary during the past ten years. The two
or three factory occupiers whom I met ' (he further
observes) ' asserted that they could not pretend
to compete with England. Manchester manu-

facturers, they said, could select their cotton on its arrival at Liverpool, close to their mills. Coal was cheaper and handier at Manchester than at Ghent. England, again, was the only producer of good machinery, and likewise possessed ready markets for her products in her vast colonial possessions. And lastly, English operatives were far superior to Flemish. On this latter point all were agreed that the Englishman, being better fed, possesses greater physical power, and produces as much work in ten as the Fleming in twelve hours, and having greater intelligence and mechanical knowledge, comprehends the machinery he works, and can point out to the foreman in case of obstruction the cause of the accident, whereas in Ghent half an hour is constantly lost in seeking for the cause of a stoppage in the machinery.

'With the exception' (continues Mr. Kennedy) 'of the long-established export trade of Belgian woollen yarn to Scotland, I may state, as the result of my inquiries, that there is little, if any, regular exportation of Belgian textile fabrics to Great Britain for consumption there. Occupiers of factories at Verviers assured me that they never exported a piece of cloth directly to England; and the same story was repeated to me by mill-owners at Ghent in regard to yarns and tissues both of flax and cotton. The reasons for the possible successful competition of Belgian with British textile fabrics must be sought for in the lower rate of wages, the longer hours of labour, and the cheaper railway transport in Belgium as compared with

Great Britain. But notwithstanding these apparent advantages, it does not appear that British manufacturers have anything to fear from their rivals in Belgium.'

Our Minister in Switzerland thus expresses himself, in his report, as to the workman in that country :

' The Swiss workman is in most respects inferior to the British workman. He has neither the physical strength nor the energy and activity of the latter. He is stolid in appearance, apathetic in temperament, slow and awkward in his movements, yet by no means wanting in intelligence. He is steady, methodical, industrious and painstaking. Though of a saving disposition, no inducement in the shape of higher wages will stimulate him to extra exertion.'

Mr. Harris, our representative in the Netherlands, reports thus :

' There is a general opinion, not unfrequently shared by the workmen themselves, that the Dutch labourer is not equal in point of skill to the foreign workman—that he is slower at his work, and turns it out in a less finished state.'

The single exception in which equality is claimed is that of the United States, where it is urged that, although the wages are higher than with us, the additional labour performed nearly compensates. As I have already intimated, I believe this statement to be erroneous where all the conditions are equal.

In 1873, Mr. Alexander Redgrave, Chief Inspector of Factories, accompanied by Mr. Jasper

Redgrave, sub-inspector, visited France and Belgium for the purpose of investigating the ' hours of labour, wages, production and like details' in the textile industries of those countries. They were armed with letters from the Right Honourable H. A. Bruce, the Home Secretary, which secured for them ' the official recognition of the French and Belgian Governments.' They instituted the most searching investigation into the questions which formed the subject of their inquiry, and the result was given in a most interesting pamphlet of fifty pages. I give the following extract from their concluding remarks :

' The value of the English workman still remains pre-eminent, though the interval between him and his competitors is not so great as it was. He has not retrograded, but they have advanced, and that advance has been chiefly caused by manufacturers importing and copying from England that machinery which supplies the place of strength, steadiness and perseverance. The Belgians are an industrious and painstaking race, but, with the French, they lack that intentness of purpose which is the characteristic of the Englishman. They are given to gossiping, their attention is not as close, they are moved and excited by more trifling causes than an Englishman. Then, again, whatever may be the proneness of the Englishman to indulgence in habits of intemperance, there is no question for a moment of the vast superiority of the cotton, woollen and flax factory operative in England over the French and Belgian workman of the same class.'

In every town the complaint against the operative was 'drunkenness.' It was difficult to make manufacturers understand that the English textile factory operatives went to their work as punctually on the Monday as on any other morning. Those who knew England were of course aware of the different manner in which Sunday is kept; but they nevertheless thought that quiet drinking would go on to such an extent on the Sunday as to make its mark on the Monday morning's work.

Although the foreign factory operative is not, as has been said, nearly so far behind an Englishman as he was a few years since, yet in all those occupations in which a call is made upon physical endurance and perseverance, the Englishman certainly maintains his pristine eminence. The Yorkshire foreman of founders who has been mentioned was certainly not backward in speaking well of his Belgian workmen, but he said they could not do the work like an Englishman; they could neither keep to their work nor do the same amount in the same time. This was a fact acknowledged by all, and accounted for partially by the difference in the nature of the sustenance of the operatives in England.

There is a striking family likeness in the allegations made by the employers of all countries against the efficiency of their workmen. In a series of valuable and exhaustive papers on the 'Wage Statistics of Germany,' by Dr. Leo de Leeuw, he shows that in various branches of the iron trade

wages advanced from 60 to 100 per cent., and in
some instances reached as high as 500 per cent.
'Yet,' he says, 'according to the unvarying testimony of the employers, the actual wages earned in
1872 and subsequent years were scarcely in excess
of the wages earned before 1867. The workmen
took the difference in idleness and dissipation ; in
most establishments it became the rule to close
from Saturday night to Tuesday morning, and
it was only on Wednesdays that work was fairly
resumed.'

I have seen extracts from the German newspapers
respecting the dissipated habits and general deteri-
oration of the German workman, that corresponded
so closely with what has been said about English
workmen, that one might have been the translation
of the other. Even the champagne story has been
current, but the consumption has been attributed,
in Germany, to the working builders, whereas in
England it was accredited to the miner.

Dr. Leeuw adduces statistics to show how large
a diminution of work accompanied the increase
of wages in the building trade of Berlin. The
following is a literal translation of his statement :

'It has lately been shown in the Berlin building
trade that the rise in wages went hand in
hand with the decrease of labour in the following
proportions :

'From 1862 to 1873 the time of work was reduced from eleven to ten hours per day ; the
day-labourer's wages rose in the same period from
1 reichsthaler to 1 reichsthaler 14.5 silbergroschen,

i.e. 50 per cent. Out of fifty buildings constructed in each year, the numbers are found as follows :

Year	Number of Days worked	Number of Stones laid	Number per Man per Day
1862	30,217	18,795,000	623
1863	31,419	21,114,000	672
1864	36,504	24,349,000	667
1865	41,305	27,020,000	654
1866	28,428	19,260,000	681
1867	26,608	17,084,000	642
1868	27,204	16,814,000	618
1869	47,599	20,230,000	446
1871	33,364	13,379,000	401
1872	36,666	12,052,300	326
1873	38,888	11,683,000	304

And now let us turn to our most eminent statisticians—men who survey the oscillations of trade from an absolutely neutral standpoint, and who have spent their lives, not in battling with more or less numerous bodies of workmen for small reductions of wage, or in minimising concessions when they are compelled to make them, but in measuring the broad results of international competition. *Testimonies to the superiority of British labour:*

I take, first, the following passage from Porter's 'Progress of the Nation.' 'The amount of skilled labour performed in a given time by any given number of our countrymen is commonly greater than that accomplished by the like number of any other people in Europe. To this circumstance it is in great part owing that, with a higher rate of daily wages paid for fewer hours of toil than are required in other countries, our manufacturers have been *Mr. Porter;*

able under otherwise adverse circumstances to maintain the superiority over their rivals.'

Professor Leone Levi; The work of Mr. Porter has been carried down to the present day by Professor Leone Levi. Confirming the favourable opinion of Mr. Porter, he describes Britain as a perfect beehive of human labour. Taking space and population into account, possibly there is no other country in the world where there is a larger proportion of labourers, where harder work is gone through all the year round, and where the reward of labour is more liberal than in the United Kingdom.

Mr. Mill; Mr. Mill summed up what he conceived to be the main features in the character of the British workman in the following passage:

'Individuals or nations do not differ so much in the efforts they are able and willing to make under strong immediate incentives, as in their capacity of present exertion for a distant object, and in the thoroughness of their application to work on ordinary occasions. This last quality is the principal industrial excellence of the English people. This efficiency of labour is connected with their whole character; with their defects as much as with their good qualities.'

Mr. Wilson; A generation has passed away since Mr. Mill placed on record the opinion I have quoted, and I find his views confirmed in the pages of Mr. Wilson, who in his valuable volume entitled 'The Resources of Modern Countries compared' has given us the latest collection of evidence on this subject. The following passage embodies the final result of Mr.

Wilson's elaborate inquiry : ' I have generally come to the conclusion that as yet our supremacy has not been substantially interfered with.   The backward wave which has swept the trade of the whole world downwards, has been due to causes too universal to lead us to suppose that any special decrease in the producing and monopolising capacity of England has occurred.   Let the conditions be the same as they are now, when business enterprise again revives, and we shall on the whole be able to retain the position we now hold.   We shall be the largest carriers in the world, the largest manufacturers, and the most extensive employers of both labour and money. The resources and advantages of the country in ships, in machinery, in mines, in skilled labour, in teeming population, in unopened stores of coal and iron, and in geographical position, are such as no other country can at present lay claim to, and with these we have nothing to fear.   Not only so, but year by year the growth of our own colonies in wealth and certain kinds of producing capacities must tend to strengthen our hands and to make the trade supremacy of England more assured.   No other country that the world has ever seen has had so extended an influence, and as yet there are almost no signs of the decay of this vast empire.'

The advantages acquired by Great Britain in international commerce during the last twenty years are shown with admirable force and clearness by Mr. Newmarch in his recent essay on ' Reciprocity.' He there shows us, to use his own words, ' why it is that since 1856 the foreign merchandise imported

Mr. New-
march ;

has risen in amount or value by 117 per cent., while the British merchandise exported has risen in value only 74 per cent., or, put in a more simple form, why it is that in 1877–75 we got 20*s.* worth of foreign goods for 11*s.*, while in 1859–56 we had to pay 14*s.* In the twenty years we have acquired such an enlarged power over the foreigner by means of accumulation of capital and improved production, that he now has to send us 14*s.* worth of his merchandise in all the cases in which twenty years ago he had to send us only 11*s.* worth.'

Mr. Wells; Again, when a note of alarm is sounded as to the incursions of the manufacturers of the United States into the Manchester markets, we may point to some examples of successful competition by British with American manufacturers. I quote the following from an essay by Mr. Wells, entitled ' How shall the Nation regain Prosperity ? ' ' In 1874 Chili imported from Great Britain more than 55,000,000 yards, and from the United States only 5,000,000 yards of cotton cloth. This little State, one of the smallest among the nations, with a population of about 2,000,000, imported more cotton cloth, to supply her wants, from Great Britain in 1874, than the United States exported that same year in the aggregate to all foreign countries combined.'

In 1874 the export of cotton goods to the Argentine Republic was in excess of 40,000,000 yards, while for the year 1875–6 the export from the United States of the same fabrics was officially reported at 155,000 yards.

Mr. Morley bore weighty testimony. 'They are turning out,' he said in a recent paper, 'a greater quantity of work in Lancashire for each spindle and loom per week than at any previous period in the history of the trade, and more than they are doing in any other country in Europe, however many hours they may work.' He reminds us that it was admitted by the Manchester Chamber of Commerce in 1876, when trade was still profitable to employers, that the price of calico was lower than in any year save one in the history of the cotton trade. Again, as he most fairly argues, 'If it were true that it is the action of the workmen that disables us in foreign competition, then we should expect that the more labour entered into the cost of production, the greater would be our disadvantage in the competition. But in the cotton trade, at all events, exactly the contrary of this is true. The articles in the production of which labour is the most expensive element are just those in which competition is least formidable. A common shirting, sold, say at 7s., and which has cost only 2s. in wages, is exposed to competition. But a piece of fine cambric, sold, say at 9s. 3d., has cost 4s. 6d. in wages, and yet in this description of goods, in which labour is the main element of cost, we have complete command of the markets.'

The 'Economist,' in reviewing Mr. Courtney's papers in the 'Fortnightly Review,' gives a more sanguine, and, as I believe, a truer view of the capabilities of the British workman than we have been accustomed to hear expressed by those who

Mr. Morley.

The 'Economist.'

O

find an easy explanation of the present condition
of trade in the increased wages and diminished
energy of our workmen. 'At this moment industries cleave to particular places in spite of equally
favourable or more favourable conditions existing
in other spots.   No reason, for example, in the way
of "cheap power" retains the alpaca trade of
Bradford in that town.   There is quite as much
"power" in Creusot, as is shown in the iron industry
of that place ;   wool and cotton are as easily pro-
curable, and the market, Paris, is, if anything, more
accessible.   Yet the mixed wool and cotton manufacture does not go there, but remains in Bradford.
There are ports in the United States which are
better fitted in all respects for the shipbuilding
trade than any ports in England, and yet shipbuilding flourishes here and does not flourish across
the Atlantic.   We do not know of any sound reason
in economics why Nottingham should beat Genoa
in the manufacture of its special fabrics.   Genoa
can obtain cotton as easily as Nottingham, and
silk more easily ;   its artisans are probably the more
adaptable of the two ;   and the difference in the cost
of the fuel used must, if we consider the minute cost
of coal-carrying and the small amount required,
be nearly imperceptible.   Nothing in the cheapness
of coal can enable English manufacturers to import
silk from Japan, manufacture it, and then sell
dresses in Yeddo of a fabric with which no Japanese
can hope to compete.   There must be something
in the English character, in its strenuousness, its love
of order, and its fidelity to work, which gives it a

superiority ; and we see no reason why this character should in any degree deteriorate. Certainly it will not deteriorate because we are nearly at the end of our resources in easily obtained coal. We incline to believe that our countrymen have been injured, if at all, by a superiority too easily acquired, and that continued adversity would develop in them an energy, industry, and power of combination with which no nation can compete, not even America, where a stimulus is lacking which is always present in England. This stimulus is want of choice. Mr. Courtney forgets that the option of working on the land, which is present to the American and the French handicraftsman, is wanting to the English. He cannot take a farm, or grow grapes, or do anything else but manufacture. He is shut up in an island so small, and cultivated on so peculiar a system, that he must manufacture or go away, and acquires of necessity the hereditary skill which in India appertains to the man who is forced by caste or opinion to continue an hereditary trade. Even if he has to import coal—and the transit of coal across the Atlantic would not greatly increase its price—he would find in his own energy the means of compensating for that outlay, as he already has done for his outlay upon food. His great competitor, the American, though quite as full of energy, has not the same inducement to expend it upon work, and as a matter of fact does not expend it. He has, for example, as Mr. Hussey Vivian says, coal and iron as ready to his hand as the Englishman. He has quite as much knowledge, and perhaps, on the whole, rather greater inventiveness. He is no further from Asia for commercial purposes, and ought, therefore, to obtain a monopoly of the Asiatic trade in small steel goods. Yet he does not, his only preference being in the axe, which, residing in a half-cleared country, he has been compelled by immediate necessity to make decidedly better than his English rival. The Englishman may of course, like the Cornish miner, be induced to emigrate, but if he does not he will retain, we conceive, a manufacturing faculty akin to his political faculty, which will still give him a fair chance in the markets of the world.'

Drinking habits of our operatives.

The opinion has gained wide acceptance that a large proportion of the earnings during the period of prosperity which preceded the present crisis was wasted in intemperance. We learn from Dr. Farr's report to the Registrar-General that during the three years of high wages in 1871–73 the consumption of spirits in the United Kingdom was 36,000,000 gallons a year. During the three subsequent years of idleness the average consumption was 42,000,000 gallons. Dr. Farr conjectures that the hours formerly spent in the workshop were passed idly in the public-house, and that this is the reason why a larger consumption took place in a period during which a very considerable reduction of wages had taken place.

Prodigality of American miners.

Complaints of the misconduct of their workmen are at least as frequent in America as in this country. Describing the cost of mining in the Lake Champlain district, Mr. Harris Gastrell states : ' The labourers

are largely foreign, Irish and others.   The miners
do not, as a rule, save.   One of their chief modes
of spending is to keep a horse and " buggy " and
drive about.   The vehicles in a miners' village were
certainly astonishingly numerous.   A library, provided for the men at a cost to each of 1s. a month,
has been given up on account of the men objecting
to the payment, and a former condition of work,
that their children should be sent to the free school
provided, has been abandoned.'

In 1860 the standard of wages was 87½ cents a
day.   It then rose to 2 dollars in 1872, and was
in 1873 2 dollars 25 cents for common labour.
It was believed that the men saved more when
paid at the rate of 87½ cents a day than they
did when the great rise in their wages had taken
place.

M. Favre admits in his reports to the Duc Drunken-
d'Audiffret-Pasquier's Commission that drunken- ness in
France.
ness, though still rare in the south, had become a
threatening scourge in the north, the east, the west,
and the centre of France.

I might have added largely to the opinions which Indige-
nous
have been quoted.   No more impartial authorities labour.
could have been consulted than those now laid under
contribution.   It was my father's conclusion, after
a long and wide experience, that in fully peopled
countries the cost of railways and other public
works was nearly the same all over the world, and
that for every country the native labour, when
obtainable, was, with rare exceptions, the cheapest
and the best.

The
English
labourer
abroad.

For a task of exceptional difficulty, one requiring all that dogged courage and determination to which Mr. Mill refers, the British miner and navvy are unsurpassed. After a long residence abroad the Englishman adopts the diet and habits of the population around him. He lives as they live, and works as they work. Climate counts for much in the physical condition of the human frame.

The preceding observations as to the uniformity observable in the cost of works do not apply to newly settled countries. Amid the sparse populations of the colonies labour is necessarily dearer than elsewhere.

Advan-
tages of
climate
and race.

I have referred to the invigorating effects of a cold climate. The influence both of climate and race is abundantly displayed in the many admirable qualities of the British people.

British
enterprise
in Cyprus.

The enterprise of our colonists and our merchants is irrepressible. During my visit to Cyprus I rode side by side with a man who had been driven only a few weeks before by the Kaffirs from his farm on the borders of Natal. He was then making a gallant effort to retrieve his fortunes in Cyprus by carrying parcels on horseback between Kyrenia and Larnaka, riding a distance of forty miles every day under a burning sun. On the following morning I purchased some Australian preserved meat from a merchant at Larnaka, who had just arrived from Vancouver's Island, where trade had been flagging ever since the island ceased to be a free port, and who had come to try his fortune in another outpost of the British Empire.

If we turn from the merchant to the manufacturer we recognise less brilliancy, perhaps, and less of that wise caution which distinguish the Frenchman, but we perceive an inexhaustible energy and admirable skill in administration.

The British workman with all his admitted faults, and notwithstanding his incessant clamour for higher wages in prosperous seasons, and his hopeless resistance to reductions in adverse times, stands before all his rivals in many essential qualities. His faults seem inseparable from the characteristic national virtues. As it has been truly said, ' On a toujours les défauts de ses qualités.'   Beaten we may be at last by the exhaustion of our natural resources, never through the inferiority of the ironworkers, the spinners, and the weavers of the United Kingdom. Their habits of industry are derived by inheritance from their forefathers, confirmed by the example of their fellow-workmen, and stimulated by emulation.   Their labours are wrought in the most favourable climate in the world for the development of the bodily and mental energy of man. *Faults and excellences of the British workman*

My knowledge of the working qualities of our labouring population has been chiefly acquired afloat, and my confidence in the British workman is strengthened by intimacy with our seafaring people. I find my own experience confirmed in a recent report from our Consul at Nantes, who gives a practical illustration of the distinguishing characteristics of the English and French seamen. An English vessel, manned by an English crew, will generally, he says, beat a French competitor out of *Character of the British seaman.*

the field, though in many ways the latter navigates his vessel more cheaply ; and why ? Because there is on board the French vessel a laxity of discipline unknown to us. Captain and crew *naviguent en famille* ; both law and custom require the captain to consult his men in an emergency.

It has often been said that the British seaman submits less readily to discipline than the Swede or the Dane, and that in the ordinary routine of a sea life he cannot always be relied upon to use his utmost energies ; but when the trial comes of nerve and strength and skill, he is rarely found wanting.

PRINTED BY
SPOTTISWOODE AND CO. LTD.,
LONDON, COLCHESTER AND ETON, ENGLAND.